feng shui

Richard Craze and Roni Jay

TEACH YOURSELF BOOKS

For UK order queries: please contact Bookpoint Ltd, 39 Milton Park, Abingdon, Oxon OX14 4TD. Telephone: (44) 01235 400414, Fax: (44) 01235 400454. Lines are open from 9.00 to 6.00, Monday to Saturday, with a 24 hour message answering service. Email address: orders@bookpoint.co.uk

For USA & Canada order queries: please contact NTC/Contemporary Publishing, 4255 West Touhy Avenue, Lincolnwood, Illinois 60646–1975, USA. Telephone: (847) 679 5500, Fax: (847) 679 2494.

Long renowned as the authoritative source for self-guided learning – with more than 30 million copies sold worldwide – the *Teach Yourself* series includes over 200 titles in the fields of languages, crafts, hobbies, sports, and other leisure activities.

A catalogue record for this title is available from The British Library.

Library of Congress Catalog Card Number: 98-67259

First published in UK 1998 by Hodder Headline Plc, 338 Euston Road, London NW1 3BH.

First published in US 1998 by NTC/Contemporary Publishing, 4255 West Touhy Avenue, Lincolnwood (Chicago), Illinois 60646–1975 USA.

The 'Teach Yourself' name and logo are registered trade marks of Hodder & Stoughton Ltd.

Typeset by Transet Limited, Coventry, England.
Printed in Great Britain for Hodder & Stoughton Educational, a division of Hodder Headline Plc, 338 Euston Road, London NW1 3BH by Cox & Wyman Ltd, Reading, Berkshire.

Impression number   10   9   8   7   6   5   4   3   2   1
Year   2002   2001   2000   1999   1998

CONTENTS

INTRODUCTION

Feng shui (which means 'wind' and 'water') is an ancient and much practised art from the Far East. It originated in China some 5000 years ago and spread throughout Asia. In the last 20 years it has spread rapidly and effectively throughout the West where many feng shui consultants have set up in business. However, feng shui is a relatively easy art to learn and, once the intuitive principles have been grasped, it is extremely simple to carry out.

In *Teach Yourself Feng Shui* we have set out to explain how the principles of feng shui work as well as giving you detailed information about how you can feng shui your own home, garden, workplace and business, as well as individual rooms.

There are some basic principles you have to learn, but once learnt you can apply them to any situation. The *remedies* needed to correct the mis-flow of any *ch'i* (energy) are simple to use and easy to acquire – you may already have some of them.

Once you learn how to direct and improve the flow of ch'i you can benefit from an improved love life, better health, enhanced luck and stable friendships – as well as furthering your career and resolving any problems you may have with your children. You may even improve your finances.

Feng shui, however, is not magic. It is based on some fundamental common sense and basic psychology. For instance, it is considered *bad* feng shui to sit with your back to a door. In ancient China this was considered as an ill omen and you were bound to suffer a *loss of face* if you did do. Obviously, we all know that if you sit with your back to a door you will feel uncomfortable as you can't see and can't know what's going on behind you. That's common sense – but it is also feng shui.

Feng shui is about putting practical common sense into a clear and coherent form so we can all benefit. Feng shui also makes you think about how and where you live. It makes you ask questions about facets of your life and suggests cures and remedies to make those facets more positive.

The effect of feng shui on your life can be likened to a torch being shone into a dark cupboard under the stairs. We know the cupboard's full of clutter and there are leaking pipes and dry rot and things that should have been thrown away a long time ago, but we aren't prepared to do anything about it – and it can only get worse. Once the feng shui torch has shown us what is wrong – and we are probably already fully aware of the problems – we simply have to put them right.

Feng shui not only illuminates the problems and highlights the dark areas but it also gives us practical solutions and instant remedies to put things right.

Feng shui is safe to practise as you can't make things worse using it. We hope you enjoy learning about it and use it wisely and well in your life.

Part One
THE PRINCIPLES OF FENG SHUI

1 | **THE PHILOSOPHY**

What is feng shui?

Feng shui is a subtle art whereby we can change our environment to alter our luck, health, wealth and love life. This may involve reorganising your entire house or merely changing where you site your desk or hanging a few mirrors in a window. As we will see in this book, the subtle change can be the one to make the most impact.

The Chinese have known and practised feng shui for around 5000 years and during that time they have had plenty of opportunity to observe the art in action to see if it actually has any benefit or positive results; if it hadn't they would have stopped doing it long before now. The fact that they haven't seems to indicate there may be something to it.

If we live our lives subject to the random forces of the universe we can't complain if we seem to suffer bad luck, misfortune, ill health and random acts of disaster. If, however, by using feng shui we decide to take responsibility and control of our lives we must surely see only an improvement. Feng shui is about taking control, taking responsibility.

Feng shui teaches us to look at every facet of our lives and question them. Are we as happy with every aspect as we might be? If we aren't then by following the principles of feng shui we can make changes. Perhaps the results of these changes cannot be as accurately predicted as we might wish but by making changes we are taking control. All the theory in the world won't change a single thing – only by actually doing something will we learn, understand and cause change. As an old Chinese sage once said:

> I hear and I forget
> I see and I remember
> I do and I understand

These changes are, in themselves, tiny but it is the fact that we are actually doing something, wresting control from fate and bestowing it upon ourselves, that has an effect. The change might appear insignificant – moving a plant, placing a mirror, hanging a wind-chime – but the results could be enormous and, of course, beneficial.

Suppose, for example, you casually throw a stick into a river. It catches on a submerged tree stump. Your stick collects other twigs and floating flotsam. This collection of debris gets bigger, becomes a dam, the river floods the neighbouring fields, drowns the livestock, forces the farmer to higher ground to take refuge, activates the emergency services. And all because you casually tossed a stick into a river.

Now suppose the river was ch'i, the universal energy, and it had flooded to such an extent that it was adversely affecting your life. A feng shui consultant might come along and say 'remove that tiny stick'. You might think it wouldn't make any difference – after all, your emotional fields are flooded, your mental livestock are drowned, your internal farmer seems to have escaped you and your emergency services (nerves) are activated – your life is dammed and flooded. You, cynically and unwillingly, remove the stick. The debris is free to wash away, the river water returns to its normal course, the fields dry out and everything returns to normal – and all because you removed a tiny stick that was clogging things up.

This example may appear trivial or irrelevant but that is how feng shui works. We clog up our lives with pieces of furniture in the wrong place or an ill-advised location for our house, or a sticking door that is hampering the good flow of ch'i. Once we unclog or remove the debris, the ch'i can flow properly again and life returns to normal. Perhaps by the judicious placing of a fresh stick we might even improve things.

Feng shui is about how ch'i flows, its strengths and weaknesses, how to improve its flow, how to control and direct it and how to make maximum use of the life-giving power it brings to us. Ch'i is like air – when it is poor quality we suffer. If we breathe good, clean, fresh air we feel rejuvenated and refreshed. If we breathe old, stale, tired air we get depressed and lethargic.

Ch'i, however, is not air – it is energy, and that energy flow has been observed, plotted, played with and manipulated by the Chinese for more than 5000 years. By learning about feng shui, we pick up on their accumulated wisdom and can use it beneficially in our own lives.

In this first part of the book we will look at the theory and philosophy behind feng shui which, by the very nature of Chinese philosophy, has to incorporate many aspects including the I Ching, Chinese astrology, Chinese traditional medicine and Taoism – the ancient religion of China, which is where we shall start.

A brief outline of Taoism

To understand the principles of feng shui we have to have an understanding of *Taoism*, the religion of China. Taoism comes from the *Tao* (pronounced: dow).

The Tao can be translated, and understood, as the Way. The Chinese say that everything is the Tao, everything is the Way. The Tao cannot really be likened to our Western concept of God except that it is all-pervading, always present, in everything and without end. The fundamental difference is that the Tao has no direct personality – it just *is*. It has no gender or agenda; no divine plan or sense of morality or sin.

From the Tao, the Way, comes everything we can know. That everything, according to the Taoists, can be divided into heaven and creation, or spirit and matter. The Taoists represented heaven as a circle and creation, surrounded on all sides by heaven, as a square (see Figure 1.1). This is a fundamental symbol often encountered in Chinese art – it is still depicted on lucky coins amongst the Chinese today.

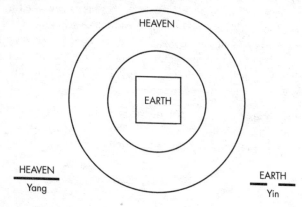

Figure 1.1   Heaven and Earth

From heaven, spirit, they reduced the circle to an unbroken line called yang, while creation, matter, became a broken line called yin. The yin/yang symbolism was further developed into the most well-known of all Chinese symbols (see Figure 1.2).

SOUTH

Yang

Heaven
South

NORTH

Yin

Earth
North

Figure 1.2 The yin/yang symbol

This is sometimes known as the T'ai Ch'i, the Supreme Ultimate or the Great Art. From the Supreme Ultimate there comes the Tao, from the Tao comes yang and yin and from those two opposites there is everything in balance. Although the yang and yin are opposites, within each there is always an element of the other. This is why there is always the tiny dot of white within the black yin, and the tiny dot of dark within the white of the yang. These two opposites are constantly being reborn as each other – in a state of constant flux and movement – and this movement between the two is what gives birth to the flow of energy, ch'i. You might like to think of it as the flow of alternating current electricity.

Yang and yin possess their own qualities and are given aspects and attitudes, but remember that this is only their basic character – they are always changing to their opposite polarisation.

Yin	**Yang**
female	male
receptive	creative
dark	light
night	day
cold	heat
soft	hard
inner	outer
down	up
north	south
matter	spirit
creation	heaven
earth	sky
negative	positive
passive	active
wet	dry
winter	summer
shadow	sunshine

This list is by no means exhaustive: everything in heaven and earth is classified, by the Chinese, as either yin or yang. The problem most Westerners have with this is that they tend to see yin and yang as two opposites; something is yin/female or something is yang/male, whereas the Chinese are always aware of the seed of the yang in the yin and the seed of the yin in the yang: nothing is ever only one or the other, there is always a balance within the thing itself.

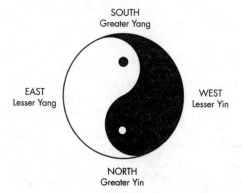

Figure 1.3   Yin/yang with compass directions

The yin/yang symbol should always be shown with the yin to the right, as shown in Figure 1.2. This is the basis of compass directions. The light yang is at the top representing summer and the south, while the dark yin is at the bottom representing winter and the north. All Chinese compasses are the opposite way round to those in the West: they have their south at the top where the Western north would be, and their west to the right and east to the left (see Figure 1.3).

Figure 1.4   Yin/yang and the human body

The yin/yang symbol can also be used to represent the human body with the head at the top representing spirit, yang, and the body below representing matter, yin. Yang is the left-hand side of the body representing male, while the right-hand side, yin, represents female (see Figure 1.4).

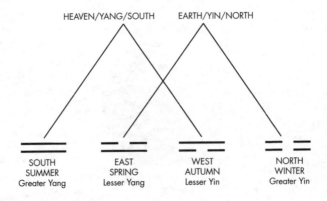

Figure 1.5   The four lines

The four seasons

Using the yin, north, and yang, south, we can combine these two symbols to create another two to represent east and west, spring and autumn (see Figure 1.5).

The eight trigrams

From these four new symbols we can then produce another four to give us the rest of the compass and the mid-season points (see Figure 1.6).

These are known as the eight trigrams (a trigram is three parallel lines).

- The top lines represent the duality of heaven and creation – the yin/yang.
- The middle lines represent heaven and creation coming together to create the four seasons and the cardinal points of the compass.
- The bottom lines represent humans.

The eight trigrams are all named and have various significance and attributes. Each is listed below, along with its Chinese name, its translation, its main attribute, direction and season.

- **Ch'ien** – *The Creative*, heaven, south, summer
- **Tui** – *The Lake*, metal, south-east, joy
- **Li** – *The Clinging* – fire, east, the sun, spring
- **Chen** – *The Arousing*, wood, north-east, thunder
- **K'un** – *The Receptive*, creation, north, winter
- **Ken** – *The Stillness*, mountain, north-west, calm
- **K'an** – *The Dangerous*, water, west, the moon, autumn
- **H'sun** – *The Gentle*, wind, south-west, wood

We can now form these trigrams into an octagon to give us the compass and the seasons (see Figure 1.7).

This is known as the *Pah Kwa*, the Great Symbol, and is probably, after the yin/yang symbol, the most easily recognised Chinese art form. It is still an incredibly potent symbol to modern-day Chinese.

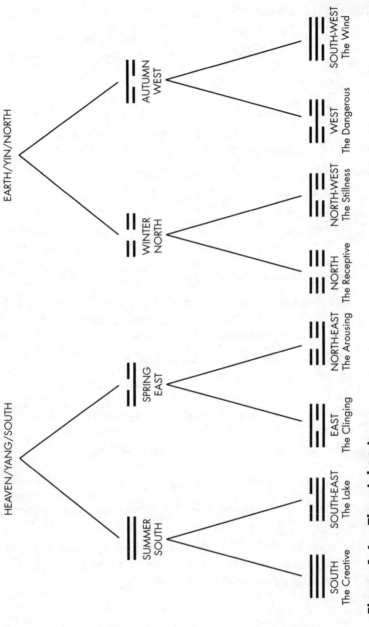

Figure 1.6 The eight trigrams

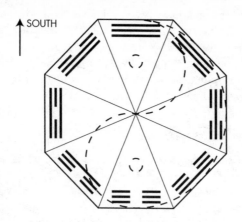

Figure 1.7   The Pah Kwa, the Great Symbol

You will notice that south is at the top, as is correct for a Chinese compass, and north at the bottom.

The eight trigrams are thought to have been developed by Fu His, a Chinese emperor, around 3000 BC. The legend tells that he first saw the eight trigrams in the ornate markings of a tortoise shell which he found on the banks of the Yellow River. The sequence in which he found them is known as the *Former Heaven Sequence*. Around 1000 BC they were re-arranged into a different sequence, called the *Later Heaven Sequence*, by Emperor Wen who was both a philosopher and founder of the Chou Dynasty. We use only the original Former Heaven Sequence for feng shui.

The I Ching

The eight trigrams can be paired into 64 new symbols (8 multiplied by 8) called *hexagrams*, which use six lines. These 64 hexagrams each have a meaning; Fu His wrote about them and used them first as an agricultural almanac which he called the *I Ching* (pronounced: ee ching), the Book of Changes. Bear in mind that this was some 5000 years ago so this is probably the oldest book in existence.

Emperor Wen added to Fu His's interpretations and turned it into the I Ching as we know it.

Today, the 64 hexagrams have become known as a sort of divination system along with Emperor Wen's interpretations, but originally the 64 hexagrams referred to compass directions and types of ch'i emanating from those directions along with what the Chinese call the eight seasons – early spring, late spring, early summer, late summer, early autumn, late autumn, early winter and late winter.

The five elements

Most Oriental wisdom, medicine and philosophy including feng shui is based on the Theory of the Five Aspects (*Wu Hsing*) which says that, whilst we are a combination of all the elements or aspects, we do tend to display predominantly the characteristics of one over the others. These elements are a sort of shorthand whereby feng shui consultants or practitioners of Chinese medicine could sum up a person quickly and accurately for the purposes of character identification – when we know who we are dealing with it makes life a lot easier.

The four cardinal points of the Later Heaven Sequence are also four elements:

- south/fire
- north/water
- east/wood
- west/metal.

The fifth element occupies the centre and is earth.

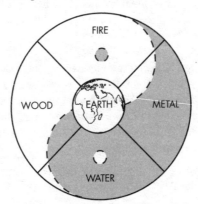

Figure 1.8   The five elements with earth in the centre

These five elements are incorporated into compass directions and human characteristics. This is why the five elements are so important to practitioners of feng shui. A consultant would want to see your house *and* know your date of birth. From your date of birth the consultant would be able to know which of the Chinese animals in Chinese astrology you are. Each of these 12 animals has five different aspects – the natural element. This element is based on the year you were born. Thus you are never just a tiger or dog or dragon but maybe a metal tiger, an earth dog or a water dragon.

Once a consultant knows which element you are they can work out which direction suits you best. Perhaps you need to know which animal you are as the animals, too, have their own compass directions as well as best seasons, times of day, key words and colours.

Chinese animals and their key words

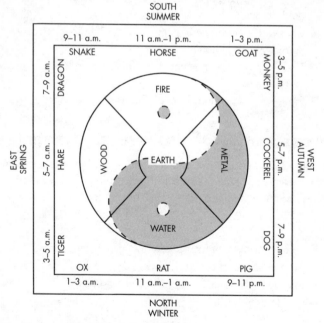

Figure 1.9 The animals and the elements

- Rat – ambitious, hardworking, determined, industrious, intelligent, practical
- Ox – patient, courageous, conventional, reliable, purposeful, intelligent
- Tiger – daring, entertaining, exhausting, passionate, dangerous, hasty
- Hare – generous, intuitive, tactile, egotistical, discreet
- Dragon – enthusiastic, daring, inspiring, successful, materialistic, independent
- Snake – intelligent, mysterious, intuitive, daring, ordered, sophisticated
- Horse – loyal, hardworking, gregarious, friendly, energetic, well-liked
- Goat – peaceful, adaptable, honest, creative, imaginative, sincere
- Monkey – independent, lively, quick-witted, entertaining, bold, inventive
- Cockerel – courageous, protective, flamboyant, capable, communicative, honest
- Dog – loyal, responsible, sensitive, moral, trustworthy, imaginative
- Pig – sensual, generous, cheerful, tolerant, fortunate, eager

Characteristics of the five elements

Each of the 12 animals has five distinct types – the five different elements – and each elemental type favours a different direction, different season and even different remedies to apply to correct any corrupt ch'i – *sha*.

Fire

- compassionate, intuitive, communicative
- likes pleasure, seeks excitement
- likes to be in love, doesn't like to be bored
- should avoid heat

Water

- imaginative, honest, clever
- seeks knowledge, original, tough, independent
- can be secretive, needs to be protected
- should avoid cold

Metal

- organised, likes to control, precise, discriminating
- needs to be right, likes order and cleanliness
- appreciates quality
- should avoid dryness

Wood

- expansive, purposeful, active
- likes to be busy, can be domineering
- needs to win, practical
- should avoid windy environments

Earth

- moderate, sense of loyalty, harmonious
- likes to belong, pays attention to detail
- likes company, needs to be needed
- can be stubborn
- should avoid damp

You can look up your year animal and element in the following chart.

1900	31 Jan 1900	18 Feb 1901	Yang	Metal	Rat
1901	19 Feb 1901	7 Feb 1902	Yin	Metal	Ox
1902	8 Feb 1902	28 Jan 1903	Yang	Water	Tiger
1903	29 Jan 1903	15 Feb 1904	Yin	Water	Hare
1904	16 Feb 1904	3 Feb 1905	Yang	Wood	Dragon
1905	4 Feb 1905	24 Jan 1906	Yin	Wood	Snake
1906	25 Jan 1906	12 Feb 1907	Yang	Fire	Horse
1907	13 Feb 1907	1 Feb 1908	Yin	Fire	Goat

1908	2 Feb 1908	21 Jan 1909	Yang	Earth	Monkey
1909	22 Jan 1909	9 Feb 1910	Yin	Earth	Cockerel
1910	10 Feb 1910	29 Jan 1911	Yang	Metal	Dog
1911	30 Jan 1911	17 Feb 1912	Yin	Metal	Pig
1912	18 Feb 1912	5 Feb 1913	Yang	Water	Rat
1913	6 Feb 1913	25 Jan 1914	Yin	Water	Ox
1914	26 Jan 1914	13 Feb 1915	Yang	Wood	Tiger
1915	14 Feb 1915	2 Feb 1916	Yin	Wood	Hare
1916	3 Feb 1916	22 Jan 1917	Yang	Fire	Dragon
1917	23 Jan 1917	10 Feb 1918	Yin	Fire	Snake
1918	11 Feb 1918	31 Jan 1919	Yang	Earth	Horse
1919	1 Feb 1919	19 Feb 1920	Yin	Earth	Goat
1920	20 Feb 1920	7 Feb 1921	Yang	Metal	Monkey
1921	8 Feb 1921	27 Jan 1922	Yin	Metal	Cockerel
1922	28 Jan 1922	15 Feb 1923	Yang	Water	Dog
1923	16 Feb 1923	4 Feb 1924	Yin	Water	Pig
1924	5 Feb 1924	24 Jan 1925	Yang	Wood	Rat
1925	25 Jan 1925	12 Feb 1926	Yin	Wood	Ox
1926	13 Feb 1926	1 Feb 1927	Yang	Fire	Tiger
1927	2 Feb 1927	22 Jan 1928	Yin	Fire	Hare
1928	23 Jan 1928	9 Feb 1929	Yang	Earth	Dragon
1929	10 Feb 1929	29 Jan 1930	Yin	Earth	Snake
1930	30 Jan 1930	16 Feb 1931	Yang	Metal	Horse
1931	17 Feb 1931	5 Feb 1932	Yin	Metal	Goat
1932	6 Feb 1932	25 Jan 1933	Yang	Water	Monkey
1933	26 Jan 1933	13 Feb 1934	Yin	Water	Cockerel
1934	14 Feb 1934	3 Feb 1935	Yang	Wood	Dog
1935	4 Feb 1935	23 Jan 1936	Yin	Wood	Pig
1936	24 Jan 1936	10 Feb 1937	Yang	Fire	Rat
1937	11 Feb 1937	30 Jan 1938	Yin	Fire	Ox
1938	31 Jan 1938	18 Feb 1939	Yang	Earth	Tiger
1939	19 Feb 1939	7 Feb 1940	Yin	Earth	Hare
1940	8 Feb 1940	26 Jan 1941	Yang	Metal	Dragon
1941	27 Jan 1941	14 Feb 1942	Yin	Metal	Snake

1942	15 Feb 1942	4 Feb 1943	Yang	Water	Horse
1943	5 Feb 1943	24 Jan 1944	Yin	Water	Goat
1944	25 Jan 1944	12 Feb 1945	Yang	Wood	Monkey
1945	13 Feb 1945	1 Feb 1946	Yin	Wood	Cockerel
1946	2 Feb 1946	21 Jan 1947	Yang	Fire	Dog
1947	22 Jan 1947	9 Feb 1948	Yin	Fire	Pig
1948	10 Feb 1948	28 Jan 1949	Yang	Earth	Rat
1949	29 Jan 1949	16 Feb 1950	Yin	Earth	Ox
1950	17 Feb 1950	5 Feb 1951	Yang	Metal	Tiger
1951	6 Feb 1951	26 Jan 1952	Yin	Metal	Hare
1952	27 Jan 1952	13 Feb 1953	Yang	Water	Dragon
1953	14 Feb 1953	2 Feb 1954	Yin	Water	Snake
1954	3 Feb 1954	23 Jan 1955	Yang	Wood	Horse
1955	24 Jan 1955	11 Feb 1956	Yin	Wood	Goat
1956	12 Feb 1956	30 Jan 1957	Yang	Fire	Monkey
1957	31 Jan 1957	17 Feb 1958	Yin	Fire	Cockerel
1958	18 Feb 1958	7 Feb 1959	Yang	Earth	Dog
1959	8 Feb 1959	27 Jan 1960	Yin	Earth	Pig
1960	28 Jan 1960	14 Feb 1961	Yang	Metal	Rat
1961	15 Feb 1961	4 Feb 1962	Yin	Metal	Ox
1962	5 Feb 1962	24 Jan 1963	Yang	Water	Tiger
1963	25 Jan 1963	12 Feb 1964	Yin	Water	Hare
1964	13 Feb 1964	1 Feb 1965	Yang	Wood	Dragon
1965	2 Feb 1965	20 Jan 1966	Yin	Wood	Snake
1966	21 Jan 1966	8 Feb 1967	Yang	Fire	Horse
1967	9 Feb 1967	29 Jan 1968	Yin	Fire	Goat
1968	30 Jan 1968	16 Feb 1969	Yang	Earth	Monkey
1969	17 Feb 1969	5 Feb 1970	Yin	Earth	Cockerel
1970	6 Feb 1970	26 Jan 1971	Yang	Metal	Dog
1971	27 Jan 1971	15 Jan 1972	Yin	Metal	Pig
1972	16 Jan 1972	2 Feb 1973	Yang	Water	Rat
1973	3 Feb 1973	22 Jan 1974	Yin	Water	Ox
1974	23 Jan 1974	10 Feb 1975	Yang	Wood	Tiger
1975	11 Feb 1975	30 Jan 1976	Yin	Wood	Hare

1976	31 Jan 1976	17 Feb 1977	Yang	Fire	Dragon
1977	18 Feb 1977	6 Feb 1978	Yin	Fire	Snake
1978	7 Feb 1978	27 Jan 1979	Yang	Earth	Horse
1979	28 Jan 1979	15 Feb 1980	Yin	Earth	Goat
1980	16 Feb 1980	4 Feb 1981	Yang	Metal	Monkey
1981	5 Feb 1981	24 Jan 1982	Yin	Metal	Cockerel
1982	25 Jan 1982	12 Feb 1983	Yang	Water	Dog
1983	13 Feb 1983	1 Feb 1984	Yin	Water	Pig
1984	2 Feb 1984	19 Feb 1985	Yang	Wood	Rat
1985	20 Feb 1985	8 Feb 1986	Yin	Wood	Ox
1986	9 Feb 1986	29 Jan 1987	Yang	Fire	Tiger
1987	30 Jan 1987	16 Feb 1988	Yin	Fire	Hare
1988	17 Feb 1988	5 Feb 1989	Yang	Earth	Dragon
1989	6 Feb 1989	26 Jan 1990	Yin	Earth	Snake
1990	27 Jan 1990	14 Feb 1991	Yang	Metal	Horse
1991	15 Feb 1991	3 Feb 1992	Yin	Metal	Goat
1992	4 Feb 1992	22 Jan 1993	Yang	Water	Monkey
1993	23 Jan 1993	9 Feb 1994	Yin	Water	Cockerel
1994	10 Feb 1994	30 Jan 1995	Yang	Wood	Dog
1995	31 Jan 1995	18 Feb 1996	Yin	Wood	Pig
1996	19 Feb 1996	7 Feb 1997	Yang	Fire	Rat
1997	8 Feb 1997	27 Jan 1998	Yin	Fire	Ox
1998	28 Jan 1998	15 Feb 1999	Yang	Earth	Tiger
1999	16 Feb 1999	4 Feb 2000	Yin	Earth	Hare
2000	5 Feb 2000	23 Jan 2001	Yang	Metal	Dragon
2001	24 Jan 2001	11 Feb 2002	Yin	Metal	Snake
2002	12 Feb 2002	31 Jan 2003	Yang	Water	Horse
2003	1 Feb 2003	21 Jan 2004	Yin	Water	Goat
2004	22 Jan 2004	8 Feb 2005	Yang	Wood	Monkey
2005	9 Feb 2005	28 Jan 2006	Yin	Wood	Cockerel
2006	29 Jan 2006	17 Feb 2007	Yang	Fire	Dog
2007	18 Feb 2007	6 Feb 2008	Yin	Fire	Pig

You will notice that the years do not correspond with our Western year beginnings and ends because the Chinese calculate their new year by phases of the moon and not at a set date.

This table also gives yin or yang aspects. You will notice that some animals are always yin and some always yang.

The yin animals are: ox, hare, snake, goat, cockerel, pig.

The yang animals are: rat, tiger, dragon, horse, monkey, dog.

Refer to the qualities of yin and yang on page 9 to see how this would influence you and your life.

Natural elements

Each animal has its *natural element* of which only four are used (not earth) and each animal has its *year element* of which there are five. Each year also has its element and its yin or yang quality.

Each animal has its qualities and needs a different living location if it is to thrive and prosper.

Fire

- Ideal house – north facing, comfortable, warm but quite grand, like a manor house
- Good interior colours – reds, oranges
- Key word – enthusiasm

Water

- Ideal house – south facing, older more traditional house, like a period thatched cottage
- Good interior colours – black, dark blues
- Key word – hope

Wood

- Ideal house – west facing, unusual, distinctive or individual like a lighthouse
- Good interior colour – green
- Key word – confronting

Metal

- Ideal house – east facing, modern, designer house
- Good interior colours – white, grey, pale blues
- Key word – organisation

Earth

- Ideal house – a mid-terrace would be perfect or a basement flat but it would have to be family oriented – perhaps a farmhouse
- Good interior colours – yellow, ochre, rust and brown
- Key word – caring

The elements for the 12 animals are:

- Water (in the north section of the compass) – pig, rat and ox.
- Metal (west) – dog, cockerel and monkey.
- Fire (south) – goat, horse and snake.
- Wood (east) – tiger, hare and dragon.

Remember here that we are referring to the animal's *natural* element – the *year* element is different. Suppose, for example, you were born in 1965 – that would make you a yin wood snake. But a snake *naturally* is a fire animal. Wood is happiest in the west (its opposite aspect) and fire happiest in the north (its opposite aspect). If you were born in 1965 you may well find your best direction would be a north-west facing home thus combining your wood and fire elements.

We look to site our home in our opposite aspect to calm down the ch'i or enliven it. For example, a fire type would seek a north-facing home so they could calm down the invigorating southern ch'i. A water type would seek a south-facing home so they wouldn't be swamped by all the protective sleepy northern ch'i.

The four compass directions

These four compass directions are important and we should look at them in some detail.

South

- Symbolised in Chinese culture by the *phoenix* – known as the Red Bird of the South
- The phoenix is called *Feng Huang* (it can also be a pheasant, cockerel or any bright bird)
- South represents luck, the summer, fame and fortune, happiness, light, joy and hope
- Its element is fire
- Animals – goat, horse, snake
- Season – summer
- The ch'i that comes from the south is *invigorating*.

North

- Symbolised by the Black Tortoise
- The tortoise is called *Yuan Wu* (can also be a coiled snake, a turtle, a black warrior and even smoke)
- The north represents the hidden, the mysterious, winter, sleep, ritual, nurture and caring
- The north's colour is black
- Its element is water
- Animals – pig, rat, ox
- Season – winter
- The ch'i from the north is *protective* and *nurturing*.

East

- Symbolised by the Green Dragon
- The dragon is called *Wen* (can also be gold but always a dragon)
- The east is protective, cultured, wise, spring, kindness and learning
- The east's colour is green
- Its element is wood
- Animals – tiger, hare, dragon
- Season – spring
- The ch'i from the east is *expansive* and *mature*.

West

- Symbolised by the White Tiger
- The tiger is called *Wu*
- The west is an area of unpredictability, even danger
- It contains warfare and strength, the autumn, anger, suddenness and potential violence
- The west's colour is white
- Its element is metal
- Animals – dog, cockerel, monkey
- Season – autumn
- The ch'i from the west is *unpredictable*.

The four quadrantal points

The Chinese actually think in terms of eight compass directions; the second four – south-east, south-west, north-east, north-west – are equally important to feng shui. They are known as the four *quadrantal* compass points.

You may be wondering why we need this information? It's all to do with the direction your house faces, which is an important part of compass feng shui.

South-east

This combines the vigorous ch'i of the south with the growing ch'i of the east to produce its own unique *creative ch'i*.

South-west

This direction combines the vigorous south ch'i with the changeable ch'i of the west to produce *soothing ch'i*.

North-east

This combines the nurturing ch'i of the north with the growing ch'i of the east to produce *flourishing ch'i*.

North-west

This combines the nurturing ch'i of the north with the changeable ch'i of the west to produce *expansive ch'i*.

As we gain or suffer depending on what sort of ch'i is arriving on our doorstep it is important to know what direction our house faces – and thus what sort of ch'i will be dominating our lives.

- South – vigorous
- North – nurturing
- East – growing
- West – changing
- South-east – creative
- South-west – soothing
- North-east – flourishing
- North-west – expansive

Once we know which way our house faces we can begin to determine which ch'i, and which quality, will dominate in our home. You may need a small compass to work out your direction.

2 | ENERGY AND FENG SHUI

Feng shui is all about energy: the energy of ch'i – how it flows, how it gets blocked, how it can become corrupted and stagnate – and what these things can mean to us.

Ch'i energy is universal; it has seasons and a flow; it has form, movement and qualities. The Chinese calligraphy for ch'i is the same as for 'rice'. Rice and ch'i are the great universal life-givers to the Chinese. As rice, the yin matter element, is cooked it gives off steam – its yang ethereal quality – which is why rice shares the same symbol as ch'i. Ch'i also plays a great part in traditional Chinese medicine. Internal ch'i has several different forms: guarding ch'i, protein ch'i, original ch'i and protective ch'i. If the internal ch'i stagnates or gets misdirected it causes illness. This illness is treated usually by acupuncture which corrects the flow of ch'i or enlivens it or slows it down by placing tiny metal needles into strategic *meridian* points along the pathways that the ch'i uses to flow throughout the human body.

Ch'i is not only internal. It is everywhere which means there is external ch'i – ch'i which is coming to us from all directions. This ch'i is affected by the direction it comes from, weather, seasonal changes and atmospheric conditions.

Ch'i and sha

If you imagine standing in the middle of your home you can turn in eight different compass directions and you will receive the benefit of the eight different types of ch'i. What if the ch'i was failing on its way to you and becoming *sha*? There are eight different types of sha depending on which direction it comes from.

Ch'i is living, bringing good energy, whereas sha is ch'i that is stagnant or corrupt and it can bring ill health, bad luck, a loss of fortune, arguments, depression and negative energy with it.

The true art of feng shui is interpreting the sha and making changes to our environment that cause the sha to become ch'i again. Once we have changed the sha to ch'i we can benefit from its positive energy again.

- ■ **South**. *Vigorous ch'i* degrades to *accelerating sha* which causes you to feel exhausted.
- ■ **North**. *Nurturing ch'i* degrades to *lingering sha* which causes you to feel lethargic.
- ■ **East**. *Growing ch'i* degrades to *overpowering sha* which causes you to feel egotistical and vain.
- ■ **West**. *Changeable ch'i* degrades to *dangerous sha* which causes you to act rashly.
- ■ **South-east**. *Creative ch'i* degrades to *provoking sha* which causes you to feel irritable and headachy.
- ■ **South-west**. *Soothing ch'i* degrades to *disruptive sha* which causes you to feel angry.
- ■ **North-east**. *Flourishing ch'i* degrades to *stagnating sha* which causes ill health.
- ■ **North-west**. *Expansive ch'i* degrades to *unpredictable sha* which causes you to feel unsettled.

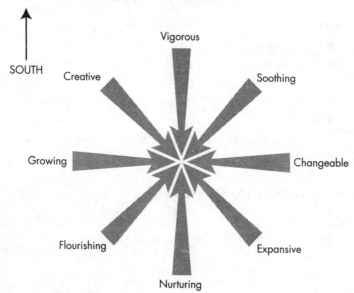

Figure 2.1   Ch'i directions

If you now look at Figure 2.1 you will see how these eight directions receive their ch'i. You will also notice that there is a definite movement from spring/east through summer/south to autumn/west and finally to winter/north.

The movement of ch'i through the year and seasons

There is a logical flow of ch'i:

- it starts as growing ch'i in the spring (east);
- becomes vigorous ch'i in the summer (south);
- becomes changeable ch'i in the autumn (west);
- and settles to sleepy nurturing ch'i in the winter (north).

The colours also follow a pattern:

- green in the spring to represent growth
- red in the summer for heat
- white in the autumn for mists and frosts
- black in the winter for sleep and hibernation.

This also gives us a cycle for the five elements:

- wood helps fire
- fire helps earth (the centre)
- earth helps metal
- metal helps water
- water helps wood.

Each of these creates the next in the cycle – but it can also hinder it if the flow is incorrect.

Ch'i and the Pah Kwa

If you refer to the diagram on page 13 you will notice that the Pah Kwa is an octagon – eight-sided. This gives us eight compass directions, eight seasons, eight types of ch'i and eight areas of life – known as the eight *enrichments* (more about these in Chapter 3).

Once we have accumulated all this knowledge we can start to practise feng shui in a very real and practical way. However, we also need to understand how feng shui is used in China and what Chinese philosophy is about. The more we learn abut China the easier it seems to incorporate the fundamental principles of feng shui into our practice.

How feng shui is used in China

As feng shui has been practised in China for at least as long as people have lived in houses, there are naturally several ancient texts apart from the books previously mentioned that outline the fundamental principles of feng shui and explain its workings, ranging from the *Shih Ching* (Book of Songs) compiled between the ninth and fifth centuries BC to the *Li Chi* (Record of Rites) developed during the Han dynasty (206 BC – AD 220).

More modern works have included the *Ku Chin T'u Shu Chi Ch'eng* (Imperial Encyclopaedia), a 1726 edition of which is in the British Museum in London, but the first reports of feng shui to arrive in the West were towards the end of the nineteenth century when missionaries first visited China on a regular basis. They were somewhat surprised to find that there was already an ancient and well-developed religion in place, Taoism, which was closely bound up with feng shui, and were somewhat taken aback when they were not allowed to erect Christian crosses. It was bad feng shui, they were told, to stab the land.

Modern feng shui in Asia

In mainland China feng shui was practised extensively until Chairman Mao's Cultural Revolution which started in 1949 and lasted for nearly 20 years when all the old culture and ways were violently discouraged by the regime. Since the easing of government authority feng shui is making a rapid return.

In Hong Kong, Singapore, Taiwan, and other places without the oppression of the Cultural Revolution, feng shui has been practised continuously. Today, it has a valid place in modern building design, and feng shui principles have been included in the construction of important new sites including the Bank of China building in Hong Kong and the Hong Kong and Shanghai Bank.

The Hyatt Hotel in Singapore reports that it is doing much better since it changed its building to improve the feng shui.

Temple feng shui

Feng shui occupies a most important part in the building of any Chinese temple. The temple has to be in keeping with the right balance of yin and yang, and it's essential that the temple is sited in exactly the right location, where it will not interfere with the ch'i, and will also fit in with the land, water, wind and various other aspects of the environment.

In a perfect world all buildings would incorporate the essential principles of feng shui. However, the demands of modern life, especially in cities such as Hong Kong, where land for building is at a premium, have led to many buildings being erected in the wrong place, or in the wrong style, or to the wrong proportions and thus interfering with the feng shui of the neighbouring buildings. However, this doesn't seem to have happened to the temples in Hong Kong; they, at least, have all been built according to correct feng shui tradition.

It is useful to understand what a building with perfect feng shui is like – you may find some features that you can incorporate into your home.

Good feng shui dictates that a temple be built on *either the pulse of the dragon or in front of a dragon stretching down from hill to sea*. This means that the temple should be built in the valley between two hills and sloping down towards the sea.

Three halls or towers

Both the inside of the temple and the outside have much attention lavished on them. The traditional Chinese temple has three halls, each leading into the other two. They don't have dividing walls. The front hall is the *bell tower*, this is where the Taoist priest keeps the temple's bell and drum. In front of the bell tower is the *smoke tower*, here are kept large urns in which are burnt the paper offerings – these have wishes and prayers written on them in traditional Chinese calligraphy. Finally, behind the smoke tower is the *main palace*. Here is where you find the altar and the images of whichever gods the temple is dedicated to. Sometimes the smoke tower has no roof but is open to the sky, much like a courtyard, to help the smoke escape. All the very ancient temples, however, have a roof over the smoke hall, which means that over the centuries the roofs have become blackened with soot. Modern smoke towers either have no roof or have ventilator shafts incorporated into them to help the smoke disperse better.

To the sides of the three halls are the *side halls*. Here the priest lives with his family.

Traditional colours

All the old temples in Hong Kong are substantial buildings of brick and stone. They are always decorated in the traditional colours of red, green, black and white. These four colours are believed to bring beneficial effects; red for happiness, green for renewal, black for comfort and nurturing, and white for peace (white is also the colour of mourning amongst the Chinese). The temples also have elaborate carvings of mythical beasts such as the dragon and phoenix. These animals are often decorated in gold to represent wealth.

Curved roofs

The roofs of the temples are curved to allow the flow of ch'i to be harmonious, and they are usually coloured green. The tiles are always made of porcelain which is made in Shek Wan, not far from Canton. These special porcelain tiles are considered an essential part of the fabric of the building and when the temple needs re-roofing they are reverently taken down, eventually to be replaced in exactly the same place as before. New temples don't have quite the same degree of lavish ornamentation but are still beautiful and elaborate by modern building standards.

The Dragon's Pearl

You may notice that on the roof of a Chinese temple there is invariably a large ball – often painted blue. This is known as the *Dragon's Pearl* or even the *Buddha's Bead*. It is, however, a Taoist symbol and nothing to do with Buddhism. It represents the cosmos – the Taoist's *blue bag*. This is an affectionate term given to the universe.

Dragons and carp

Either side of the Dragon's Pearl you may see a dragon or a carp. These two bring good luck and protect the temple from any evil influences that may be circulating above the roof. The dragon is a benevolent beast of great wisdom and protection. The carp is, of course, a baby dragon. That is why the carp is so important to the Chinese as both a real fish to be kept almost as a pet, and as a symbol of success overcoming adversity. The carp, having to swim upstream and across weirs and waterfalls to mate, has become a powerful symbol of achievement, ranking as an equal with the dragon in Chinese culture.

The Flaming Pearl of Wealth

You may often see a small ball in the mouth of carved stone dragons. This is placed there as one of the Taoist's Eight Great Treasures. If you watch the famous dragon dance performed on New Year's Day by the Chinese it is always led by a dancer holding a large red ball to signify the Flaming Pearl of Wealth.

Carved lions

The temples often have carvings of lions. This may seem strange as the lion is not indigenous to China; it was introduced by the Buddhists who arrived from India. The lion was always placed at the entrance to Buddhist temples as a protector, and the Taoists added the lion to their list of protective animals. The lion was said to suckle its young with its magical claws which spouted milk. The lions are playful creatures who like to play with balls and that is why in China you'll often see them carved with a ball between their front paws. Simple folk in the country leave a hollow ball out at night for the mythical lions to play with in the hope that their claws would puncture the ball and leave behind in it some of the magical milk which had properties that could confer longevity on anyone who drank it.

Lions versus tigers

You will hardly ever see a Chinese tiger protecting a temple, or even a home. The tiger is much more dangerous, a beast to be placated rather than used as a guardian. The tiger is a symbol of unpredictability and change; the lion one of friendliness and protection. The tiger is very much a Taoist symbol; the lion, although originally Buddhist, has now been adopted by nearly all the Chinese schools of philosophy.

The ancient wisdom of the East

Feng shui is now taking its rightful place in the West, with increasingly more people realising its importance and validity. We all have to live in a dwelling and it makes sense to make them as comfortable and harmonious as possible. If we can adapt principles from another culture and incorporate them into our lifestyle to make our living more prosperous and beneficial, then it makes sense to do so. There is a lot of ancient wisdom from the East that is being recognised as worthwhile and can help us in many ways.

How feng shui is used in the West

Many businesses operating in both the East and West now see the value of feng shui principles being incorporated into building design and décor. They include Citibank, Morgan Bank, Chase Manhattan and the Asian Wall Street Journal offices.

In the United Kingdom the house building firm, Wimpey Homes, has issued a 12-page 'beginner's guide to feng shui' for prospective purchasers of new homes. Their feng shui-inspired advice includes injunctions to treat your home as an expression of yourself and to love it as such; to bring nature into your home so that you are never the only living thing in the house; to provide a personal retreat or sanctuary in the home and have a natural gathering place as a communal space. It adds that the colour yellow is a good colour for this space, in a picture, bowl or vase of flowers. Yellow is associated with relaxation and nurturing – it also represents the centre, which is where a communal space should be as it shares all the compass directions. The guide also says that first impressions are important, so keep the outside neat and tidy.

Wimpey says a lot of interest has been registered by Japanese customers in the feng shui of its Britannia Village development in the Docklands of London. Wimpey Homes are not alone: other companies who practise feng shui principles in their businesses include Marks and Spencer, Virgin Atlantic, the Ritz hotel chain, and the Orange mobile phone network.

Another company in the United Kingdom which is embracing this ancient art is the B&Q Warehouse, home improvements chain. When B&Q opened its first warehouse in the Far East, in Taiwan, the General Manager, David Inglis, became intrigued: 'at first I thought it was just rather amusing, but when I saw how deeply the Taiwanese believed in it, and how strictly they made feng shui principles a way of life, I began to read more about it and became more deeply interested myself,' he said.

Feng shui hasn't reached only companies. Many successful and famous people are now incorporating feng shui principles into their own homes. They include Richard Branson, the late Diana, Princess of Wales, Donald Trump, Michael Caine, Anita Roddick and Boy George.

Shipping tycoon Tung Chee-hwa who is the head of Hong Kong's first post-colonial government has claimed that the feng shui in Government House in Hong Kong is not good: 'I've heard it is very crowded.' He is still undecided about whether he wants to move in – or whether to turn it into a colonial museum.

Summary

You have had to learn a lot of information in this chapter – and there's more to come, but once this information has seeped in – and it doesn't take long – you can begin to put some of it into practice. The information you need that is relevant to you, without having to learn the whole lot, is:

- Your Chinese animal – and element and yin or yang type. You obtain this from the year of your birth (look at the chart on pages 17–20);
- The direction your house faces – you obtain this by opening your front door and seeing what direction you are facing. If you are unsure, check it with a compass.

Now you know what you are and where you are (according to Chinese philosophy) we can go on to the next chapter to determine what you are going to do with this information – how feng shui works in practice.

3 | PUTTING FENG SHUI INTO PRACTICE

The eight enrichments

In Chapter 2 we learned how much of Chinese compass feng shui fits the concept of everything being divided into eight areas – eight compass directions, eight seasons, eight types of ch'i, eight types of sha. It also incorporates the eight main areas of our lives – fame, wealth, health, wisdom, friends, family relationships, children and pleasure.

If we refer back to the octagon we can see that the eight compass directions are each influenced by a particular type of ch'i. Each type of ch'i governs or influences a different area or *enrichment* of our life. These enrichments take into account virtually every facet of life that we need to be able to perform as successful satisfied adults. You can see that if the ch'i from a particular compass direction has become sha then it will adversely affect that area.

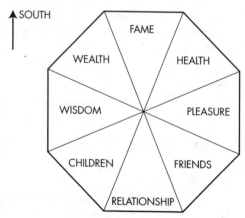

Figure 3.1   The eight enrichments

The Pah Kwa

This octagon with its eight enrichments is called the Pah Kwa (it is sometimes spelt *bagua*) and it works for an ideal house – that is, one that faces south.

However, if your house faces east or north, we move the Pah Kwa round to face that direction. The fame enrichment is always positioned over your front door.

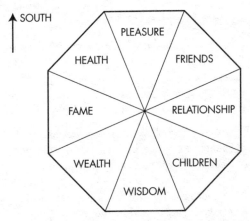

Figure 3.2   Pah Kwa with east-facing house

We need now to look at these eight enrichments to see how they affect our lives and why the differing ch'i affects them. You'll notice that each of these enrichments is numbered. We'll find out why below.

- Fame – 1
- Wealth – 8
- Wisdom and experience – 3
- Children and family – 4
- Relationship – 9
- Friends, new beginnings – 2
- Pleasure and indulgence – 7
- Health and happiness – 6

The lo shu magic square

If you draw the Pah Kwa as a square the numbers form a *lo shu*, or magic square. Add the numbers in any direction and they add up to 15. The lo shu is an ancient Chinese device used for all sorts of ritualistic magic purposes and its layout is incorporated into many building designs. It is also valuable for *walking the Nine Palaces* which is a ritualistic way of checking the feng shui of a building, which we look at later in this chapter.

8	1	6
3	5	7
4	9	2

Figure 3.3   The lo shu magic square

These eight enrichments are important to feng shui and we need to look at each in detail.

Fame

Fame, or reputation, is the area from which you step out into the world, where you present your 'face' to the rest of the world. Your fame enrichment is influenced by what is immediately visible as you open your front door. What do you see? Hopefully a 'good' view – one that is invigorating, hopeful and inspiring – because this is how you will perceive the world. Open your front door on to 'negative' views such as seedy back streets, factories or rubbish dumps and that will affect your dealings with the outside world. Your emotional horizons are influenced by what is outside your front door – the wider the view the greater your scope for coping with what the world can throw at you. The more limited and narrow the view the more subject to stress and 'loss of face' you will be. The area of your fame enrichment is not only what you can see outside your front door but also what you have immediately inside it. What have you got there?

Traditionally in Western homes, this may well be an area where you keep the equipment you need to step out into the world – your overcoat, umbrella, keys, etc. It's also the area where the world comes in to you. How the world perceives you is influenced by how you approach the world. Step out from your front door boldly, full of confidence and hope and that is how the world will greet you. Step out sadly with your head down and the world will treat you accordingly.

Ideally, your fame enrichment should have elements of the colour red in it. Red is bright and full of life – fire to motivate you in the world. This is the area of the Red Phoenix – the bird of recovery. No matter how bad things have been, when you step out from your fame enrichment there is always hope of rebirth – a new start. No matter how low you've been brought, you can always rebuild, start again.

What ch'i comes from the south? Vigorous ch'i – ch'i to make you feel fired up and ready to take on the world, ready to enhance your fame, improve your 'face' and spread your reputation successfully. Vigorous ch'i degrades to accelerating sha. This can cause you to feel exhausted – it all becomes too much for you and you can't go out because the world seems too much effort to take on. Accelerated sha needs to be remedied to make it vigorous ch'i – we will find out how to do this later in this book – so you can take on the world again, full of renewed vigour.

Wealth

Your wealth enrichment is the second most important area, according to traditional Chinese feng shui, and this is the second most auspicious place to have your front door. Your wealth enrichment is where you find your magnet to attract money. Look at the area to the left of your front door (looking from the inside). What have you got there? This is what is affecting your money-earning potential. Is this a good area? Is it full of light and beauty or dark and ugly and unused? How's your bank balance? Beautiful or dark? Your wealth enrichment benefits from creative ch'i – it creates wealth as it arrives so you may need to check what the ch'i is passing before it arrives in your wealth enrichment. Creative ch'i degrades to provoking sha. This can make you irritable – it can also cause you to spend money too freely on things you don't really need or want. It literally provokes you and you react by trying to buy peace of mind. It's a sort of 'I can't cope so I'll go shopping to cheer myself up' approach to life. We all suffer from it at some time. If it is a serious habit you may need to remedy this area. If money slips through your fingers faster than water then you need to look closely at this area and see what is causing this. Perhaps there's a small downstairs cloakroom here with a dripping tap or leaking pipes?

Health and happiness

Your health is the enrichment to the right of your front door. Ideally, it will face south-west, ready to benefit from the soothing ch'i that flows from this direction. Soothing ch'i helps your health by easing your stress. It also enables you to find peace and happiness here. This should be an area where you can relax and take time out; an area just for you, dedicated to your own needs during quiet times. What have you got here? How do you think it might affect your health? Soothing ch'i degrades to disruptive sha. This can cause you to feel angry – and anger is a symptom of stress. How can you relax and enjoy peace and happiness if you're always feeling angry? Check this area carefully and make sure it is comfortable and relaxing, ready to benefit from the soothing ch'i.

Wisdom and experience

In Chinese culture the dragon is a symbol of wisdom and benevolence and the Green Dragon lives in the east. What better place to have your wisdom and experience enrichment, where it can benefit from all that dragon energy? Ideally, here you'd have well-rounded green hills – the back of the sleeping dragon – and in the enrichment you'd provide a place to study and keep your scholastic honours. What do you have in your wisdom enrichment? In the West, education is considered to cease when a person leaves school whereas the Taoists see it as an ongoing process – the longer we live the more we need to know, and the longer we have to learn. For the Chinese growing into wisdom is as important as is being rich in the West. Being wise lasts longer, is less subject to a recession, benefits those around you more and helps you find satisfaction in your life more fully. Without wisdom and experience we cannot mature and grow – and pass on that wisdom to our children, helping them to take their place in the world.

Your wisdom enrichment benefits from growing ch'i – and you grow in wisdom and experience every day. The dragon is the symbol of spring; each day has the potential to teach you more than you knew yesterday, to grow in stature and maturity. Growing ch'i degrades to overpowering sha which causes us to feel egotistic and vain.

Pleasure and indulgence

Your pleasure enrichment is the area governed by the White Tiger – unpredictable and potentially dangerous. Ideally, to the west of your home you'd have a small lake surrounded by wildflowers to calm the enormous power of the Tiger. Too big a lake and the Tiger will devour you; too small and there will be no excitement in your life. Your pleasure enrichment is the area where you entertain, if that's how you seek your pleasure. It's an ideal place to have your dining room where you can serve delicious meals to your friends and indulge yourself. We all need to be indulged from time to time and your pleasure enrichment is the place to do it. It benefits from changeable ch'i – we wouldn't want all pleasure, all indulgence, but we do need it occasionally. Changeable ch'i is unpredictable – like the power of the Tiger – and can turn to dangerous sha easily, which can cause us to act rashly – perhaps drink a little too much or take things too easily and become lazy. The blowing wind of changeable ch'i refreshes us and keeps us on our toes but too much and we can feel unsettled; this is what causes the rashness. This is not a place to make decisions or to negotiate contracts but rather a place to unwind and enjoy ourselves.

Relationship

Traditionally, this enrichment is the area that relates to marriage. However, in the West there is a tendency towards 'relationships' rather than marriage so that is how we will refer to it. Your relationship area should be situated in the north, ideally. The Chinese believe that a successful marriage is very important. How can you find satisfaction in this world without your soul mate, your ideal partner? Once we have found such a person, we have to look after the relationship to make it work. We have to protect it and care for it or it will fail. Relationships benefit from the nurturing ch'i of the north but if it is allowed to degrade to lingering sha it causes lethargy – and that is the biggest cause of failure in any relationship. If we don't work at it and endeavour to keep it fresh and exciting it will atrophy and die. It makes sense to keep the area of relationship at the back of the house, in the north, to protect our loved ones and keep them safe. This is why your children and family enrichment is also here. Ideally, we'd have the black hills of the Tortoise behind us to protect the most vulnerable members of our family. Your relationship enrichment is traditionally associated with an area of warmth and sleepiness. Here we can have the family fireside and enjoy the nurturing ch'i.

Children and family

This is the area in which to feed young babies, to keep a comfortable chair by the fire to read stories to children, even keep the television if that's what it takes to keep the children entertained. What do you have here? Your children enrichment benefits from flourishing ch'i, and what could be better for growing offspring? However, it degrades to stagnating sha which is a cause of ill health. Check this area carefully if you want your children to flourish and not suffer from endless colds and the sort of minor irritations that affect infants. Your children enrichment enjoys both the nurturing power of the Black Tortoise and the wisdom of the Green Dragon and that is probably all that children really need for them to flourish and grow healthily and well. Your children enrichment is probably the most protected area and that is where children need to be, safe and secure nestling between the sleepy hills of the north and the wise hills of the east.

Friends, new beginnings

Your friendship enrichment is the ideal area for sounding out new ideas, new projects. Here you can discuss your plans for the future, prepare for your holidays, chat to friends and get their advice. This is an enrichment where improvements in your life will begin. It benefits from expansive ch'i combining the nurture of the north with the change blowing in from the west. A good place to dream a little, to wish a little, to allow your imagination to take wing and chance all those plans you'd never dared hope for. Keep a note pad and pen in this area and you will always be getting new ideas here. Write them down before you forget them. Your friends will gravitate naturally towards this area when they visit; keep a bottle of good wine here and they will enjoy that expansive ch'i. Limit them a little or you'll find you're sitting up half the night talking new plans and ideas. Watch the expansive ch'i, though, as it degrades to unpredictable sha. If left unchecked or unremedied, it can cause friends to suddenly stop dropping in, or your plans to come to nothing – or to be altered into something you *didn't* want. Unpredictable sha causes you to feel unsettled and restless. You begin to feel overwhelmed – what's the use of planning anything if nothing ever happens?

The eight remedies

It seems logical that if there are eight compass directions, eight types of ch'i, eight types of sha and eight enrichments then there will be eight remedies – and there are, of course.

For ch'i to bring you health and good fortune it must be allowed to flow in its natural way – this is in smooth curves and at the proper speed. Too fast and it will cause disruption and allow anger to manifest. Too slow and it will stagnate and cause lethargy and depression. Ch'i likes to flow gently through open spaces and if you provide clutter and untidy areas it will become confused and unfocused. Ch'i likes harmony and beauty, cleanliness and balance.

You should be aware of what the ch'i has flowed through or near before it arrives at your home as it is liable to pick up residues of any unpleasant occurrences. Ch'i dislikes straight lines that cause it to pick up speed and flow too quickly. It also dislikes being trapped in small confined areas. When you walk the nine palaces, which we will do later in this chapter, you imagine yourself being the ch'i and you can ask yourself if you too could flow smoothly through your home or would you be obstructed, confused, confined, accelerated or stagnated? If you find that the ch'i is not being allowed to flow as freely as it needs to, then you may find it manifests in your life as lack of money, an unfortunate relationship, an inability to relax, loss of friends, noisy and badly behaved children or even, perhaps, ill health. If the ch'i is being impeded in any way you will need one of the eight remedies which are:

- light
- sound
- colour
- life
- movement

- stillness
- functional objects
- straight lines.

Light

This includes lights, mirrors and reflective surfaces. Mirrors are probably the most widely known feng shui remedy. They can be used in most situations. They will reflect bad ch'i, sha, back out of a building, encourage good ch'i to flow in by capturing a pleasant view from outside, lighten and enlarge small dark rooms, deflect ch'i around hidden corners, even alter and change the psychology of a room. Used in conjunction with lamps, mirrors can transform a room completely. Lights should be as bright as possible without causing glare. You should never be able to see a bare bulb. The Chinese use a lot of lights outside the house and in the garden to fill in missing or dead ch'i. It's not something Westerners tend to make use of but lights can enhance a dull garden, especially at night.

Traditionally, in China, special octagonal mirrors have always been used to deflect unpleasant ch'i back to where it has come from. The mirrors are placed facing outwards towards whatever it was that was regarded as incorrect. You can use any small mirror to do the same. If your house faces a graveyard or factory then a small mirror placed to reflect the sha will improve the ch'i entering your home. Any dark areas or corners of your home can be livened up by placing good-quality lamps in them. Soft lighting is best to create harmony. You can also use mirrors to encourage light into darker areas or placed at the end of long corridors to slow the ch'i down. Light remedies are traditionally associated with your *fame* enrichment.

Sound

Most people associate Chinese culture with wind chimes without realising that they are an important feng shui remedy. Anything that makes sound can also be used: bells, metal mobiles, bamboo tubes, etc. Melodic noises can help to break up stagnant ch'i by causing swirls and eddies of sound in the air. Wind chimes also act as gentle alarms to tell us when someone has entered our house. Pleasing and harmonious sounds are also good attractants of lucky ch'i: they are said to encourage wealth into buildings.

The sound of water flowing is beneficial. Fountains can be seen as both movement and sound.

Harsh noises cause ch'i to become jangled and inharmonious. You can use wind chimes, bells, even the sound of water fountains to create a harmony of sound and soothe the the ch'i. Sound remedies are traditionally associated with your *friends* enrichment, so you can play music here to provide your guests with harmonious sound.

Colour

The Chinese are great believers in using colour to stimulate the flow of ch'i, especially the four dominant colours of red, white, gold/green and black. These are lucky colours associated with attracting fame, activity, wisdom and wealth. In the West more subtle colour schemes are generally preferred, but it is useful to remember that a sudden patch of bright, strong colour in a stagnating room can stimulate ch'i effectively.

Any area where you feel stressed or irritable should be decorated simply in pale colours, white is best, and then a single, simple flash of bright colour introduced to focus the ch'i and keep it vibrant. Colour is traditionally associated with your *children* enrichment since it stimulates them – that's why children's toys tend to be such bright colours.

Life

Plants are mainly used to fill in blank areas where there isn't any ch'i or to help ch'i that is stagnating to 'come to life' again. They can be used to hide disruptive, sharp corners that poke into rooms and stimulate ch'i in areas where it might linger. Large plants can be used to slow ch'i down when it is being directed too quickly along straight lines. Fish in aquariums are also used for the same purpose. The Chinese for 'fish' and for 'money' is the same word so they often use fish to represent wealth. That's why you will often see fish tanks next to the cash register in Chinese restaurants – it encourages you to spend freely.

When ch'i is weakening or causing a depletion of energy or life force you need to introduce some element of life into an area. Pot plants are best but they should have rounded leaves. Cut flowers aren't a good idea as their ch'i is leaking away as they die, and dried flowers are frowned on as they have no life left in them. Plants should not be left untended or allowed to get dusty. Traditionally, plants are associated with your *wealth* enrichment. The Chinese use fish in tanks to introduce life into an area. If you want to do the same you should keep an odd number of fish: goldfish are recommended.

Movement

Wherever ch'i needs to be stimulated or deflected, use a moving object. The Chinese use flags, silk banners, ribbons, fountains, wind chimes, mobiles and weather vanes. Moving objects should use the natural power of the wind if possible and be made of natural materials.

The smoke from incense can be regarded as movement and be used beneficially but obviously only short term.

Flowing water brings ch'i to the building but it should move gently and gurgle rather than roar. An ideal location for a house is one where it faces south with a babbling brook in the south-east bringing in lots of money.

Movement is associated with your *relationship* enrichment and this is where we need movement to stop things getting stale and being taken for granted.

Stillness

Any large inanimate object such as a statue or large rock can bring stillness to an otherwise too-fast ch'i area. This is especially beneficial in gardens where the path to a front gate can cause the ch'i to leave too quickly. Any statues used should blend harmoniously into your home and have a particular significance for you. You can use large natural objects like driftwood or a bleached, gnarled branch.

In China, there is an area in the home where a statue is placed to provide a focus for spirituality. This is often a Buddha but you could use any large, beautiful object. It should be simple but exquisite and it will slow ch'i down and help to purify it. Traditionally associated with your *pleasure* enrichment, a still object will allow you many happy hours relaxing and contemplating natural beauty or the perfection of a craftsperson's labour.

Functional objects

In traditional feng shui, this usually meant machinery or tools but nowadays it can be extended to include any electrical equipment used in the home: televisions, stereos, electrical fans and, probably most important of all, computers. Electricity and ch'i need to be harmoniously regarded if they are not to clash: both need to be treated with respect. Electrical equipment can stimulate ch'i but sometimes it can overstimulate it, so keep it to the minimum.

Anything functional or manufactured that does a job of work, or is a tool, can be used to stir up dull ch'i – anything from a refrigerator to an electric kettle. You need to be careful not to overdo it as functional devices tend to be strong remedies. Traditionally functional objects are associated with your *wisdom and experience* enrichment so this is a perfect place to keep your computer.

Straight lines

The Chinese use flutes, swords, scrolls, bamboo tubes and fans to break up ch'i when it moves heavily or sluggishly, especially along beams and down long corridors. The straight lines are hung at an angle to create the Pah Kwa octagonal shape and that helps to direct the ch'i away from the beam or corridor and back into the rooms.

Although we have talked of ch'i disliking straight lines, there are times when ch'i needs to be enlivened or interrupted. Perhaps you have beams that ch'i can flow along too quickly; you can use anything that has straight lines in it such as the items described above to break up the ch'i and deflect it into the room. Straight lines are traditionally associated with your *health* enrichment.

Using remedies

Here are some tips on how to recognise when you need to apply a remedy. Check each of the eight areas of your life. How are your finances? Your relationship? Your health? Your fame and reputation? Check each one in turn. If you are happy with that particular area of your life then the chances are that you don't need a remedy there. But, if you are experiencing problems, you may need to do some work on that area. Let's suppose it's your finances that are suffering a bit. You check the area and find that your money enrichment happens to fall in your dining room. Perhaps you've been eating all your money? If you visit a Chinese restaurant you may see, as we said earlier, a fish tank near the cash register

– this is to encourage money to come to life. Perhaps you could try placing a fish tank in your dining room? Or a large plant to encourage the ch'i to provide good fortune?

Suppose it's your relationship area that is suffering and you check that enrichment area to find that it falls in your study. Perhaps you have been devoting too much time to work? Or are you and your partner in business together and you don't spend enough time together away from work? You could try introducing a wind chime above your desk to stir the ch'i up, or how about one of those executive desk toys that moves? Or if you have your computer here, try running a moving 'screen saver' when you're not using it.

The thing to remember with remedies is that you can't do any harm by introducing one into an area. If it's the wrong one you will simply remain static – there'll be no improvement. Sometimes you have to experiment and move things around before you produce a positive result.

What ch'i likes and dislikes

Remember that ch'i likes:

- harmony
- gentle curves
- beauty
- spaciousness
- order.

Ch'i dislikes:

- disorder
- clutter
- straight lines
- neglected areas.

Sometimes you have to completely revamp your house – not because the decoration is wrong but because decay and neglect have set in. Ch'i likes spring cleaning and freshness. Sometimes that's all you need to do to an area to benefit from better ch'i – tidy up and spring clean. Our homes should reflect the inner self. If we are cluttered and confused inside, our home will reflect that. By clearing out the debris externally we can shift the inner clutter and revitalise ourselves. By focusing on a particular enrichment of our life we have already taken a major step towards improvement.

The eight remedies and their ideal enrichments

Each of the eight remedies has a particular enrichment area in which it works best:

- Light – associated with your *fame* enrichment
- Sound – associated with your *friends* enrichment
- Colour – associated with your *children* enrichment
- Life – associated with your *money* enrichment
- Movement – associated with your *relationship* enrichment
- Stillness – associated with your *pleasure* enrichment
- Functional objects – associated with your *education* enrichment
- Straight lines – associated with your *health* enrichment.

Those are the basic principles upon which feng shui is based. It's a lot of information to take in at once so it might help to remember it in easy stages.

As a reminder there are:

- eight compass directions
- eight types of ch'i
- eight types of sha
- eight remedies
- eight enrichments.

These all fit together rather like a jigsaw puzzle. If one of them is 'wrong' or out of place it can throw everything else out. By correcting the faulty piece, the rest falls into place and life becomes smooth and successful again. Identifying the fault and correcting it is – feng shui.

Which way does your house face?

There are eight different directions in which your house can face. Remember the direction is set by the direction of your front door. You may use a side entrance, climb in through a window, swing down from the roof – and it won't make a bit of difference. The house direction is set by the front door direction. If you look out of your front door and find yourself facing west, you have a west-facing house. If you are facing the north-east, you have a north-east facing house. If you choose to use another entrance then that says something significant about you and your dwelling; this is one aspect you should look at carefully. Perhaps if you use a different entrance – such as a side entrance – you may be seeking a different enrichment as the dominant one, or a different ch'i to work with, or even a different element type to live with. We will explore this more later.

Before we look at the different house directions there is an interesting part of feng shui about yin and yang that you may have already noticed from the previous chapters, but it needs emphasising. There are four yang directions and four yin directions.

The four yang directions

- East
- South-east
- South
- South-west

These four directions correspond, in the ideal favoured south-facing house, to four enrichments:

- wisdom and experience
- wealth
- fame
- health and happiness.

These are known as the *four personal enrichments*. These are all yang, all corresponding with the 'male' principle; the 'I' part of life. They are concerned with the individual; your own personal wisdom, wealth, fame and health.

The four yin directions

- West
- North-west
- North
- North-east

These four yin directions correspond, in an ideal south-facing house, to four yin enrichments:

- pleasure and indulgence
- friends and new beginnings
- relationship
- children and family.

These are the four yin enrichments. They correspond with the yin or 'female' principle. They are all to do with 'us'. They are known as the *four collective enrichments*.

You may have noticed the *four yang personal enrichments* are all located at the front of the house whereas the *four yin collective enrichments* are located at the back of the house.

- The front of a house is *yang* – personal – confident – bold – outward.
- The back of a house is *yin* – collective – nurturing – protective – inward.

It's an interesting part of house design that if you want to know the true history of a house always look first at the back. The front is usually changed a lot. New frontages are added on and fashions change. The front is a visible sign of an occupant's personality. The back, however, undergoes less change. The front may be radically altered but the back will remain much the same as when the house was first built. The back is less visible so is less subject to fashion but it is more representative of the inner personality of a house.

Yin and yang aspects of the home

The front, yang aspect of a house is usually where the car is parked – a visible sign of the occupants being out in the world. The back is where the occupants relax in private, where they play with their children. A visitor coming to the front door rings a bell and waits for someone to answer. But what if the same visitor walks unannounced round to the back and straight into the back garden or door? How would you feel? Would it be a shock to your system? An intrusion on your privacy? The visitor has invaded your yin and disturbed you. The same visitor coming to the front door is respecting the yang and is welcomed. I'm sure you can think of other examples of this.

By now, you may be thinking that your house doesn't face south and therefore can't be ideal. The word 'ideal' isn't ideal. The early feng shui practitioners recommended that a house should face south and based all their calculations on that. It is a most beneficial direction and if they were consulted before a house was built would always recommend it. You probably bought or rented your home long after it was built and therefore inherited its direction without thinking about it. Perhaps subconsciously you selected a different direction, because each of the eight directions does actually suit different people.

Walking the Nine Palaces

In China when a house was first built no one would live in it until the local Taoist priest had been along and blessed it. The priest would probably have been instrumental in helping with the design of the house anyway. The priest would *walk the Nine Palaces*. This entails walking through the house according to a ritual which is based on the *lo shu* – the magic square (see Chapter 2). You should always use this ritualistic way of walking through your home whenever you need to check any of the enrichments.

Walking the Nine Palaces mentally fixes what you are actually doing. This isn't a casual stroll through your home wondering if you need to redecorate. You are following an ancient way and those who have gone before you would appreciate your time and respect in continuing the tradition.

Taking your time

In the West we tend to rush at things too much. Walking the Nine Palaces is an Eastern philosophy and one that goes on at a slower pace. Take your time and enjoy the journey. If you rush through walking the Nine Palaces you may miss that tiny detail that will change things for you. It's very easy to think we 'know it all', that all we have to do is have a quick check and everything will be fine. If you rush this walk, you don't allow your home the space to speak to you, to tell you what it feels is wrong and what it would like corrected. Feng shui is not an exact science, it can't be proved by reason or logic. It functions on a different level from anything else we've ever encountered and we need to open channels into our intuitive nature. The Taoist priests knew this and when they walked the Nine Palaces with the house's new owner they would take their time, stopping in each enrichment to allow the owner and the house to get acquainted, to become one with each other. In each enrichment they would have lit some incense and burnt paper prayers – these were written in traditional Chinese calligraphy on rice paper and they flare up quickly, the burnt embers rising upwards taking the prayer heavenwards.

Your living home

In the West, many people feel that a home is just somewhere to rest up for a while before going back to work. In China, a home is seen as a living being. It needs breath and life for it to enrich us and protect us properly. If we neglect our relationship with our home then we will be that much poorer in spirit for it. Feng shui is about relearning things we may have forgotten. The fabric of the building is as important as the decor; the decor as important as the furnishings; the furnishings as important as the light, air and breath of the house. All of these are as important as us, the living occupants of the house.

Recently, in the West, some research has been done on the effects of living under or near overhead power lines and electricity pylons. Evidence does seem to point to the fact that living in such locations is injurious to health. Feng shui would have told you that without any research being done, papers compiled, scientists involved, doctors consulted or anyone having to be at risk. If we all live according to stricter feng shui principles and respect the landscape and environment, the pylons would never have been erected in the first place and no one need have suffered.

The nine questions

Back to the Nine Palaces. You start at your front door which we will call **1**. At each enrichment stop and listen. As you are walking the Nine Palaces you need to ask nine questions in each enrichment.

- How does this area feel to you?
- How do you feel about it?
- What would you change in this enrichment?
- What feels right here?
- What feels wrong?
- What problems have you encountered in your life that relate to this enrichment?
- What can you take away from this area?
- What is missing from this area?
- If you were starting from scratch would you have this area the same as it is now?

Your front door is **1** – your fame area. Open your front door, look out and ask the nine questions. When, and only when, you are satisfied with the answers move on to the next area. Imagine that Taoist priest is standing with you and asking the questions. What answers would you give? Perhaps you might like to do this exercise with someone you really trust, someone whose advice and guidance you respect. Get them to ask you the nine questions. Your answers may sound different if you have to say them out loud. It's as if having to justify the answers to another person has the capacity to make us really sure of what we feel and say about a particular area.

Once you have finished with your assessment of your fame enrichment, then you can move on to **2** – friends and new beginnings. You will find this area immediately to the right at the back of your home – the back right-hand corner – assuming, as we will for all these directions, that you are facing the front door. Once you have asked everything here you can move on. Sometimes walking the Nine Palaces can take quite a while. You should allow at least a whole day for this – you inevitably get side-tracked, caught up in examining the tiniest detail of not only how and where you live but also why and what for. The nine questions may spark off all sorts of unexpected lines of enquiry – so take your time, this is nothing to be rushed.

Move on to **3** – your wisdom and experience enrichment. You will find this along the left-hand side of your home. Again, ask the questions and when you are ready move on to **4** – children and family. You will find this immediately behind your wisdom enrichment. These two enrichments are connected, they flow into each other. Remember that your *children* may not be your physical offspring, although your children enrichment is usually taken to mean just that. In this area you should again ask the nine questions and be satisfied with the answers before you move on to **5** – the centre of your home.

Jen Hsin – the centre

This is not an enrichment but it is known as *Jen Hsin* – which can only really be translated as *heart of the heart*. This is the very centre of your home, the heart, and it deserves special consideration. If you are not sure exactly where the centre of your home lies then perhaps it may be worth measuring it. You can pace out two diagonal lines between the four corners of your home and then where they intersect will be Jen Hsin. Once you've found it you have only to see what you've got there to recognise what your home revolves around. This is the pivot, the centre, and your home, possibly your life, revolves around this heart centre. If you are unhappy about what you have here, or you feel that this is not the right thing for your home to rotate around, then change it. Replace whatever you have here with something more suitable. This is quite a surprising exercise to do and you may be in for a shock when you discover what it is that forms the heart centre of your home.

Continuing the nine questions

Once you have finished here you move on to **6** – your health, peace and happiness enrichment. You will find this area to the right of the front of your home – the right-hand corner, if you like. Again, ask the nine questions and, when you are ready, you can move on to **7** – pleasure and indulgence. This area is the right-hand side of your home, directly behind your health enrichment. While you are checking out your pleasure and indulgence enrichment you can sit down here and see if this area really is as comfortable as it ought to be.

Once you have finished being comfortable you can move on to **8** – your wealth enrichment. This is the left-hand corner of your home. Again, ask the nine questions and when you are ready move on to **9** – relationship. This is the back of your home, nestling between children and friends. Perhaps here you should be asking the questions with your partner.

Once you have finished with 9 – relationship, you should go back to 1 – fame. Here you should again check everything is in order. During the walking of the Nine Palaces you may have changed many things and you need to check that the first area is still in harmony, in balance, with all the changes you have made.

From yang to yin, from yin to yang

You may have noticed that as you walk the Nine Palaces you are constantly crossing from a yang area to a yin area, and back to a yang area. As you move between yin and yang, yang and yin, see how the mood of each area changes. Yin areas should be as light and bright as possible; yang areas can be darker and quieter. The principle of yin and yang is that they always seek the opposite – so you can provide it by knowing which each wants to be in harmony.

The eight-pointed star

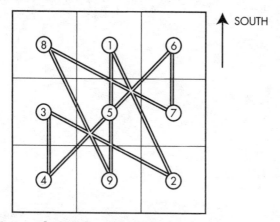

Figure 3.4   The eight-pointed star

You may also have noticed the shape of the ground plan you are tracing as you walk the Nine Palaces. This strange eight-pointed star shape (see Figure 3.4) is designed so that you cross and re-cross each area the same number of times and so that you always move between yin and yang. The order you are walking, in terms of enrichments, is fame to friends to wisdom to children to health to pleasure to wealth to relationship, and back to fame. The order you walk the Nine Palaces in terms of compass directions is: south to north-west to east to north-east to south-west to west to south-east to north, and back to south for a south-facing home. Obviously if your home faces a direction other than south, the compass order will be different.

4 | THE MECHANICS OF FENG SHUI

Making the home pleasant and harmonious

As we spend most of our time at home it makes sense to ensure that it is as pleasant and harmonious as possible. In the West, decor and interior design are used for that, while in China feng shui is used as well. The Chinese are as concerned as Westerners to ensure that the visual impression is pleasing but they also like to make sure that the energy flow in and around the home is as beneficial as possible.

Key areas to check

We need to check a few key areas when we apply feng shui to our homes. If we work through them in order it will make it easier for you to remember when you come to apply the principles to your own home:

- mountains
- surroundings
- water
- wind
- trees
- dwelling
- inside
- ourselves.

Mountains and surroundings

If you do not live near mountains, the principles of feng shui can still apply if you consider any tall buildings near you as 'mountains'. Their towering presence can overpower your ch'i. Concave and convex mirrors can turn their image upside down which will negate the effect of their powerful ch'i. Similarly, the reflection from a bowl of water will have the effect of flattening their image.

Any tall buildings should, ideally, be in the Tortoise and Dragon areas – to the north and east. If they are not, you will have to flatten them – with mirrors, of course – to make flat zones in your Phoenix and Tiger areas, to the south and west. Place small mirrors in the window facing outwards.

'Surroundings' means checking the immediately surrounding neighbourhood for good or bad feng shui. What are the neighbours like? Are there ugly buildings close to you? You need to look out from the eight cardinal points of your home to see what is there. You also need to check the eight types of ch'i that may be directed at your home.

Start by physically standing outside your home in each of the eight cardinal compass points and look to see what is there.

For example, you may stand with your back to the side of the house that faces south and find yourself looking at a particularly unpleasant factory. Is this really where you want your vigorous yang ch'i to come from? What about the side of the house facing the factory? Is it your main entrance or a blank wall? If it is blank then the factory ch'i will not do too much damage but what if it is your front door? What if the factory makes armaments or weapons of some sort, or uses dangerous chemicals? What sort of effect do you think *that* ch'i would have on you and your life?

East

Stand and look east from where the growing ch'i is coming. This ch'i stimulates you, gives you your creative energy. So what's there? Another factory? A splendid view of rolling hills? Which would you prefer?

North

Look to the north, the direction of nurturing ch'i. This is the sleepy stuff that you can roll up in and hibernate. Ideally, it should undulate down from the Tortoise hills in a gentle embracing way. What have you got there?

West

To the west is the changeable ch'i. It is disruptive and unpredictable. The Chinese sometimes say it is dangerous and destructive. Where's your west ch'i coming from? How is it getting into the house? Is this your main entrance or a back door that you hardly ever use? If it is the main entrance you need to deflect it firmly. Use the largest mirror you can on the inside wall immediately opposite the door so that the sha is deflected straight back out again. If it is a back door you can use a smaller mirror or wind chimes to break up the sha as it enters. If you don't use the door too much then it's not so imperative to deflect the sha. What windows open on to the west? Have a look and decide how much sha can get in through them. You can deflect sha by hanging small balls of glass in the window to spin round on thread and give off prisms of colour as they catch the light. The Chinese traditionally used to black out any west-facing windows.

South-east

This is where your creative ch'i is coming from. What's there to stimulate your creative processes?

South-west

Soothing ch'i comes from the south-west. But is it soothing? It will pick up a lot from whatever it passes through or over just before it arrives at your home.

North-east

Flourishing ch'i comes to us from the north-east.

North-west

This is the home of expansive ch'i, but if it has passed over or through anything unpleasant it can cause us to feel extremely unsettled when it reaches us.

Terraced houses

Obviously, if you live in a semi-detached or terraced house you can't do this test on all walls.

If you live in a terrace, the ch'i coming from your neighbours is important. You can also go to each end of the terrace to see what is coming towards the whole line of houses.

Tower blocks

If you live in a block of flats or high-rise building, you have the added complication of what is coming up from below. Maybe you live above a shop. What sort of shop? What sort of ch'i is filtering up through your floors? The Chinese would never live above a funeral director's but might be very happy to live above a bank.

Basements

Living in a basement, a very yin place, needs consideration as to what is above you. Again it may be shops or other flats. The Chinese feel that any place that may have been subject to emotional distress, like a police station, a prison, army barracks or hospital, gives off a particular type of ch'i called *fan ch'i*, translated as *offensive ch'i* and it can be harmful, causing you to feel the same emotional distress as was originally generated.

Feng shui and harmony

A lot of feng shui is intuitive work. We can't give examples of every type of house and the direction it could face. You have to look yourself and feel whether the energy is right. A lot of feng shui is also common sense. If, every time you open your front door, you are confronted with a dreadful view you are bound to feel worse than if you look out on a wonderful vista of countryside, streams and beautiful hills. Your quality of life improves with the quality of your horizons. You might think you can't control your view – but you can. You can usually choose where you live and when to move or what to do to remedy anything wrong. It's your choice. Feng shui is about taking responsibility; feng shui is about waking up to choice. You can improve your surroundings but ultimately you may have to move if you come to realise that where and how you live is adversely affecting your emotional and spiritual horizons.

Some people, however, can resist negative forces better than others – you're perfectly entitled to live opposite a factory if you choose – just be aware that you're making that choice.

We need to look for harmony in our lives, to seek out the natural and the nurturing. If we choose to live in an inner city surrounded by derelict buildings, busy, polluted roads and millions of other people then we are going to feel the effects that all that negative ch'i generates. If we choose to live in the countryside in quiet, tranquil surroundings with beautiful views then we will benefit. Obviously there has to be, as in all things, a question of balance. There will always be a time in our lives when we need the excitement and stimulation a city offers and a time when we need to get away from it all. Judging when those times are, is up to you. Only *you* can tell when you have had enough and need to recharge. A lot of people, however, don't even think about the alternatives. Feng shui is about seeking that balance, that harmony.

Water and wind

We need water around us. If we haven't the privilege of living near a river or stream then we have to add the water ourselves. That's why aquariums are so important to the Chinese.

Water carries ch'i as well as being a soothing element of our environment. If there are rivers and streams near us we need to look at the way they will bring ch'i to us. Using the principles that we have already learnt we can work out which are good and which are bad. Ch'i, which is beneficial, likes to meander; sha, which is disruptive, likes to travel in straight lines. So, does the river head straight for your home or wander happily around it? Is it a gently babbling brook or a concrete-banked canal? Guess which carries ch'i and which carries sha. It's time for you to do some work now.

Do you look out over a lake? Large bodies of water such as lakes, reservoirs, even large ponds, accumulate ch'i. Is it overwhelming? Even worse, is it in the west? A lake here would store sha in large quantities and would almost certainly be an extraordinarily powerful force that would erupt unpredictably.

Is the lake in the north? This could make you very sleepy.

We need water in the home and if we can use mirrors to reflect watery views inside, so much the better. The sight and sound of water moving naturally can be most beneficial and soothing.

Trees

The Chinese word for trees in a feng shui context is *liu* which is directly translated as 'willow'. The willow is the tree most often represented in traditional Chinese landscape paintings (which are called *shan-shui*, incidentally). If we see buildings as the yang element of the landscape then trees are the yin: and we need both for our spirit to be nurtured. The shan-shui painters work on a ratio of 3 to 2: three yang elements to two yin. They also see, as do feng shui practitioners, hills as yang and hollows as yin. If you take a panorama, three-fifths should be yang, the sky, and two-fifths yin, the landscape. We can use yin trees to balance an excess of yang buildings or yang hills. In the West this ratio is also used and is known as the 'golden section', a proportion as important in Western art as it is in Eastern. Liu, trees, can also be understood as 'garden'.

Dwelling

This is the feng shui of the actual building itself: the walls, the windows, the doors, the rooms and the decor. We will look at this in greater detail in Part Two of this book.

Ourselves

There is little point in getting the feng shui right if the heart of the home also needs work doing on it. We can see ourselves as the heart – the *jen hsin*. We need to be as in balance as our home. Getting the feng shui right can make quite a difference but we also need to sort out our own personal feng shui. We are the recipients of all that good ch'i. We have to put ourselves in a position to make good use of it all. Correcting the feng shui and leaving ourselves out of the equation is pointless. The original feng shui practitioners were also Taoist priests. As well as correcting the feng shui of the dwelling they offered advice to the home owner on health and spiritual matters. They corrected any faults with *jen hsin* as they went along.

Assuming you have your own home and are not looking to move at the moment then you can work through the feng shui of your home in an ordered fashion. Here is a checklist to remind you:

- The eight directions
- The five elements
- The eight enrichments
- The nine palaces
- The nine questions

The eight types of house

As we move the Pah Kwa round to face the compass direction your house faces, it will be apparent that there are eight basic house directions. Each of these eight house directions has eight enrichment locations – and consequently benefits from the eight types of ch'i in different ways. For instance, if you have a north-facing house your fame enrichment will not face south but north. The north brings nurturing ch'i. How do you think that will change your reputation or career? Obviously, it will have an effect – and may direct you to working in a more caring profession such as counselling or medicine. Your wisdom enrichment would be in the west – subject to that changeable Tiger ch'i. How would this affect your learning powers? The west is an unpredictable area where we cannot anticipate or plan because we are always subject to the vagaries of fate. Perhaps if you have a north-facing home your wisdom becomes erratic or subject to fits and starts.

Suppose you had a south-west facing home, and you were concerned about your health. Look where your health enrichment falls – in the west again. This could cause your health to be unpredictable – unless you remedy it.

We will now look at the eight different house types.

The south-facing house

This is a very yang home – vigorous, creative – out in the world full of energy and light.

1 **South – fame enrichment**. Your fame benefits from vigorous ch'i but can suffer from accelerating sha. This is an area that benefits from lots of light – this shines on your fame like a spot-light – or the flash of a camera.

2 **South-east – wealth enrichment**. Your wealth benefits from creative ch'i but can deteriorate into provoking sha. As you have a south-facing house you probably work in the public eye, perhaps in some creative field?

3 **East – wisdom and experience enrichment**. This is enjoying growing ch'i and should continue to do so unless it degrades to overpowering sha. This area needs a serious functional object to enhance all that wisdom and help you gain experience.

4 **North-east – children and family enrichment**. Here you can enjoy flourishing ch'i. A good place for you to be but how sure are you that you can cope with the noise? This is

the area of the thunder; it's arousing and colourful but if neglected the ch'i becomes stagnating sha.

5 **North – relationship enrichment**. This is where your relationship is supposed to be – quiet and sustaining, in the north area of your home and life. The ch'i here is nurturing and you can be enveloped in warmth, love and comfort. If you neglect this area, the ch'i becomes lingering sha which can make you question everything too much.

6 **North-west – friends and new beginnings enrichment**. This is an area enjoying expansive ch'i, but the ch'i can become unpredictable sha. You need to incorporate the stillness of the mountain that symbolises the north-west into this area. You also need to fill this area with sound to harmonise the sha.

7 **West – pleasure enrichment**. The ch'i here is changeable and needs to be calmed and balanced with a stillness remedy.

8 **South-west – health and happiness enrichment**. The ch'i here is soothing and needs to be encouraged with straight lines. This area is gentle like a soft breeze and can bring you great peace and good health.

The south-east facing house

This is the home of the entrepreneur and the businessperson. It's a very yang house, full of being out in the world – and the front door opens straight out into the wealth enrichment – good for making money.

1 **South-east – fame enrichment**. Here you step out of your front door straight into the wealth and possessions area of life. This is your area. Here you are happy. What could be better than enjoying all that creative ch'i and using it to make yourself richer and your family better off? However, creative ch'i can become provoking sha. You should settle this area, if it has become problematic in any way, by using a combination of life and light.

2 **East – wealth enrichment**. Your wealth will come from what you already know – this is a wealth enrichment in the east which is your experience. The ch'i here is growing. The ch'i here can become overpowering – fill this area with life and functional tools.

3 **North-east – wisdom and experience enrichment**. Here you have a yang enrichment benefiting from yin flourishing ch'i. The ch'i can become stagnating sha which can stop any further growth in your wisdom enrichment. You need to combine both colour and a functional object in this area.

4 **North – children and family enrichment**. A good yin enrichment in almost its ideal location. Here the ch'i is nurturing which makes you protective towards your family. However, the ch'i can become lingering sha which could make you overprotective. To counteract this you should incorporate both movement and colour.

5 **North-west – relationship enrichment**. This is a yin enrichment in the yin compass direction of north-west – which is traditionally associated more with friendship than with marriage. The ch'i here is expansive.

6 **West – friends and new beginnings enrichment**. The ch'i here is changeable which can cause your friendships to come and go without warning. Remedy this area with both sound and stillness.

7 **South-west – pleasure enrichment**. A good yin enrichment facing the best yang direction it could – the ch'i here is soothing which couldn't be better for relaxing and indulging yourself.

8 **South – health and happiness enrichment**. If you don't feel healthy with this yang enrichment in such a vigorous yang compass direction then perhaps you are suffering from accelerating sha. Try remedying this with a combination of straight lines and light.

The east-facing house

This is a yang house of someone who likes being out in the world but only to explore, to find out how the world works rather than to take from it.

1 **East – fame enrichment**. When you step out of your front door into your fame area it is into the east, the traditional home of the benevolent Dragon who guides and offers great wisdom. Your reputation may well be, as is the ch'i from the east, growing. Caution should be exercised lest it becomes overpowering sha. Fill this area with light and functional objects.

2 **North-east – wealth enrichment**. Here a typically yang enrichment enters a yin compass direction. The ch'i here is flourishing which means an accumulating wealth enrichment. The ch'i can become stagnating sha if the learning is not being passed on to enough people.

3 **North – wisdom and experience enrichment**. Here your wisdom enrichment is in the north and needs assistance from your partner. This is a good balance of a yang enrichment in a yin compass direction.

4 **North-west – children and family enrichment**. If you want your parenting to be relaxed and happy then you couldn't choose a better direction to be in. The ch'i here could become unpredictable if left unattended. Make sure this area has lots of sound and colour.

5 **West – relationship enrichment**. A yin enrichment in a yin compass direction ought to provide you with good beneficial ch'i but it is changeable – coming from the White Tiger. It can quickly become unpredictable – and extremely volatile. Fill this area with stillness and movement in equal quantities.

6 **South-west – friends and new beginnings enrichment**. The south-west brings soothing, gentle ch'i which will help your friends bring you great peace of mind. The ch'i can become disruptive sha unless remedied.

7 **South – pleasure and indulgence enrichment**. The ch'i can become accelerating here which can exhaust you. Deflect it with stillness and light – or at least turn it aside before it totally drains you.

8 **South-east – health and happiness enrichment**. This is a good yang enrichment in a good yang location. Here your health is benefiting from creative ch'i and should bring you joy.

The south-west facing house

This is the house of someone who uses their caring, nurturing side to help others.

1 **South-west – fame enrichment**. This is the most yin of the four yang directions. When you step out into the world you step out into the soothing wind of the south-west and you find your fame helping others to overcome their difficulties which will probably be associated with their health – and that can be physical, emotional, or even spiritual.

2 **South – wealth enrichment**. The south is known as the creative heaven direction, full of invigorating ch'i. If the ch'i shows any tendency to become accelerating sha – and you can tell if it has become so from the amount of clutter you keep in this area – then remedy it with life and light.

3 **South-east – wisdom and experience enrichment**. This is a good yang enrichment in a good yang compass direction. Here your wisdom can benefit from creative ch'i. If the ch'i becomes provoking sha you will have to fill this area with plants and a functional object.

4 **East – children and family enrichment**. This is a yin enrichment in a yang compass direction – the balance, however, is good with your family benefiting from growing ch'i from the benevolent wisdom of the Dragon. The ch'i can become overpowering – fill this area with bright, colourful, functional objects.

5 **North-east – relationship enrichment**. Here your relationship is benefiting from flourishing ch'i which can be arousing, but the ch'i can stagnate very easily. All you have to do is stir it up with lots of colour and movement.

6 **North – friends and new beginnings enrichment**. Here your friendships benefit from nurturing ch'i. Any friendships forged here will last a long time. This is a good yin enrichment in the best yin compass direction for protection and caring. If the ch'i becomes lingering you can help it along with movement and sound.

7 **North-west – pleasure and indulgence enrichment**. Here your pleasure enjoys expansive ch'i. What a good place to relax in and enjoy being you. If the ch'i becomes unpredictable sha you can make it more harmonious by using sound and stillness.

8 **West – health and happiness enrichment**. Here the ch'i is changeable and needs to be watched carefully. This is a yang enrichment in a volatile yin compass direction. The power of the Tiger can be unleashed suddenly and unpredictably and become dangerous sha all too easily. This area needs straight lines which run at right angles away from the west (i.e. north to south) as well as stillness.

The north-facing house

What a good place to have your fame enrichment – your loved ones must know you to be the most caring, sensitive and considerate person there is.

1 **North – fame enrichment**. This is where you are in the world – stepping out with your loved one on your arm. Don't you just feel that everything is right with the world when you are in love? This is the most yang of enrichments in the most yin of compass directions. If the ch'i becomes lingering sha, remedy this by filling this area with movement and light.

2 **North-west – wealth enrichment**. Your finances may grow and shrink with alarming regularity. Settle this area with life and sound.

3 **West – wisdom and experience enrichment**. A yang enrichment in a changeable yin compass direction. If you want to settle the sha here then use a functional object combined with a stillness remedy.

4 **South-west – children and family enrichment**. This is an area of angels and beasts. One minute everything is perfect and the next it's the end of the world. To pull the two extremes towards each other you could use straight lines and colour in this area.

5 **South – relationship enrichment**. The most yin enrichment in the most yang location. Here's the place for a creative, vigorous relationship indeed. If the ch'i becomes accelerating sha, remedy this excess of energy with lots of light and movement.

6 **South-east – friends and family enrichment**. Your friendships enjoy the creative ch'i from this compass

direction – they'll always find new ways of cheering you up when your love has left you. Remedy this area with life and sound.

7 **East – pleasure and indulgence enrichment**. Some people like to switch off when they relax and do nothing – but not you. However, if you find it difficult to completely unwind then use this area to contemplate on a beautiful practical object.

8 **North-east – health and happiness enrichment**. If you can balance this yang enrichment with the yin flourishing ch'i you can enjoy only good health. However, the ch'i can stagnate and you may find yourself depressed by it. Remedy it with colour and straight lines.

The north-east facing house

This is known in Chinese feng shui as the Dragon's lair house. The home of the Dragon indeed, and dragons can't help but give advice – it's what they're there for.

1 **North-east – fame enrichment**. This is the enrichment where you step out into the world – and your world is populated with lots of people seeking advice, help, leadership, and your time and attention. If the ch'i here stagnates too much you may actually be doing nothing. Enliven it with light and colour.

2 **North – wealth enrichment**. One of your great dislikes is listening to advice from others. Fill this area with life and movement if you want the lingering sha to return to being nurturing.

3 **North-west – wisdom and experience enrichment**. Keep it simple. Keep it accurate and don't try to teach anyone anything unless they ask. Keep this area from becoming unpredictable by using sound and functional objects.

4 **West – children and family enrichment**. Children like provoking the Dragon and making it roar, and what better place to do it than in the opposite location for it to feel any peace. Remedy this area with colour and stillness.

5 **South-west – relationship enrichment**. Here you can be soothed by all that south-west ch'i. This is a good yin enrichment in a gentle yang location. Your relationship may well benefit from being a work partnership as well. If the ch'i becomes disruptive sha, remedy it and provide yourself with a more peaceful relationship by adding movement and straight lines.

6 **South – friends and new beginnings enrichment**. What a good place to have your friends enrichment. It's a good yin enrichment in a very positive yang location. If anyone tries to hurry you too much then the ch'i has become accelerating sha and you'll need to slow it down by using light remedies and sound remedies.

7 **South-east – pleasure and indulgence enrichment**. This is the place where you should relax and unwind. What have you got here? Is this area benefiting from all that creative ch'i? Or is it being wasted? Is this an area that provokes you? Or that won't let you rest here? Then remedy it with lots of plants and beautiful statues.

8 **East – health and happiness enrichment**. The ch'i here is growing – and it comes from the east, the spring. This is excellent for your health. You can recover quickly, improve your stamina and maintain good all-round health here. If the ch'i becomes overpowering sha you may be tempted to take on too much and exhaust yourself. Remedy this by incorporating a functional object with lots of straight lines into this area.

The north-west facing house

This is the house of someone who looks out for others – care workers and police officers favour the north-west facing home.

1 **North-west – fame enrichment**. When you step out of your front door you step into the north-west. This is all to do with looking after other people. If the ch'i becomes unpredictable sha and you find yourself getting irritable, then remedy this area with light and sound.

2 **West – wealth enrichment**. Your finances, facing in this direction, must be so changeable you wonder if you'll ever be straight money wise. If your finances ever look like becoming a severe problem, then the ch'i has become dangerous sha and you'll need to fill this area with lots of life.

3 **South-west – wisdom and experience enrichment**. You can learn from your mistakes – unlike some other people. If the ch'i becomes disruptive sha then remedy this area with straight lines and functional objects.

4 **South – children and family enrichment**. This is a perfect place for a parent to be. You have limitless energy and great skill at entertaining small people. You delight in small children. If the vigorous ch'i becomes accelerating sha you may find yourself exhausted, so remedy it with lots of colour and light in this area.

5 **South-east – relationship enrichment**. A good yin enrichment that benefits from the creative ch'i of a yang location. If your relationship becomes provoking then remedy this area with lots of plants and lots of movement.

6 **East – friends and new beginnings enrichment**. It doesn't take you long to bounce back from adversity, nor does it take you long to make new friends and settle into new situations. If the ch'i becomes overpowering, remedy this area with functional objects and sound.

7 **North-east – pleasure and indulgence enrichment**. Here you can relax in warmth and comfort. A good yin enrichment in a good yin location. The ch'i here is flourishing and you should be able to relax easily. If the ch'i becomes stagnating sha, remedy it with lots of colour and stillness.

8 **North – health and happiness enrichment**. You may be prone to injury – only because you rush at everything so eagerly. This enrichment is a good place to recuperate; it's quiet with yin, nurturing ch'i to heal and help you. If the ch'i has become lingering sha you will need to remedy it with movement and straight lines.

The west-facing house

This is the house of the greatest pleasure lovers – and all to do with food.

1 **West – fame enrichment**. As you step out of your front door you step into the great pleasure areas of life. This is the location of changeable ch'i, which means you like variety. You enjoy all the pleasure that this world can offer but if the ch'i becomes dangerous sha the pleasure will turn to over-indulgence. If that happens fill this area with light and stillness.

2 **South-west – wealth enrichment**. Too much wealth would unsettle you despite what you think. This south-west wealth enrichment will bring you enough but not too much. The ch'i here soothes rather than inflates. Should it degrade to sha it will be disruptive and you may find your finances cause you more problems than you anticipate. Remedy this area with lots of life and straight lines.

3 **South – wisdom and experience enrichment**. Your wisdom enrichment is in the south which is the most yang of yang locations. This is where we get the most vigorous ch'i from and it can overwhelm us if we are not sure enough of our experience. If the ch'i is allowed to become accelerating sha, fill this area with light and functional objects.

4 **South-east – children and family enrichment**. Good place to be if you like children. They may provoke you, though, with their messy habits – so remedy this provoking sha with lots of life and lots of colour.

5 **East – relationship enrichment**. The strongest yin enrichment in a yang location. If you enjoy and learn from growing within a relationship then this is a good area for you. Fill this area with movement and functional objects if you feel overwhelmed.

6 **North-east – friends and new beginnings enrichment**. A perfect place for you. This is where you should entertain all those friends of yours. Good place for your dining room. If the ch'i becomes stagnating sha, you'll have to remedy this area with colour and sound.

7 **North – pleasure and indulgence enrichment**. If your kitchen is in the east and your dining room in the north-east, then what could be better than having your sitting room here in the north? This location is very yin, nurturing and warm and here you can unwind. If the ch'i is allowed to linger here you'll never move. Remedies are to have movement and a beautiful piece of sculpture.

8 **North-west – health and happiness enrichment**. Watch your weight. The ch'i here is expansive and so could you, too, expand. To remedy this, fill the area with sound and straight lines. If the ch'i is allowed to become unpredictable sha who knows what could happen – it's unpredictable.

Overlaying the Pah Kwa

Now we've looked at the different directions your house could face we have to look at which bits of your house are missing. First, we need a ground plan of your house. This could be a simple sketch, a rough outline. It doesn't have to be anything too elaborate. Once we have a ground plan we can overlay the Pah Kwa on to it. If your house is roughly a square shape, the Pah Kwa will cover the outline of the house. But what if your house is 'L' shaped? Or very long and thin? Once you've overlaid the Pah Kwa on to the ground plan, you'll find it doesn't fit without distorting it. We are interested in which bits are missing – or which bits you have too much of.

Any extra bits of house are enrichments that you have in abundance – perhaps too much abundance – only you can tell. Any enrichments that are missing are the ones you don't have. The enrichments should each occupy about an eighth part of your life if you are to have harmony and balance.

If any enrichments are missing then you can hang large mirrors at the point where the enrichment would begin – this works for enrichments that are too small as well. This will give the illusion of the enrichment being there – or being larger. Hopefully this will enhance that area of your life so that you obtain the elements or qualities of that enrichment.

Any enrichments that are too large should be closed down by lowering the lighting levels or restricting the ch'i by using straight-line remedies to stop the ch'i expanding in that area too much.

In Part Two we will look at how you can check the feng shui in individual rooms and in your garden as well as at work and in business.

Part Two
APPLYING THE PRINCIPLES

5 | FENG SHUI IN THE HOUSE

We've already looked at how your house or apartment fits into its external surroundings; this chapter is about the inside of your home. We'll look at its shape and what that can tell you, and then we'll look at each room in turn to see how you can get the maximum benefit from the feng shui.

The layout of your home

In Chapter 4 we talked about the Pah Kwa and about establishing which way your home faces. In order to work out the feng shui of your house, you now need to overlay the Pah Kwa on to a plan of your house. Take a plan – it can be fairly rough – and place the Pah Kwa over it so that the front door is in the fame enrichment of the Pah Kwa. You can now read off which enrichment each room or area falls into (see Figure 5.1).

If you are concerned about any particular aspect of your life, you now know which part of the house governs it. Suppose money is your big worry. If your wealth enrichment covers the bathroom, for example, this is clearly the room on which to concentrate.

Sometimes you may even be able to swap rooms around to improve things. Suppose one of your children has a tendency to ignore school work in favour of socialising, listening to music, or any other form of enjoyment. Maybe their bedroom falls in the pleasure and indulgence enrichment, which is encouraging this lifestyle. Perhaps you could move them into the wisdom and experience enrichment, by swapping their room with the spare room, or with another child who is prone to be workaholic, or changing where they do their homework.

Some rooms are just too difficult or too expensive to move around, such as bathrooms and kitchens, in which case you can look for remedies within the rooms, as we shall see. But you can move most rooms around to place each in a more appropriate enrichment. You may be able to swap sitting rooms, dining rooms, bedrooms and studies around quite easily.

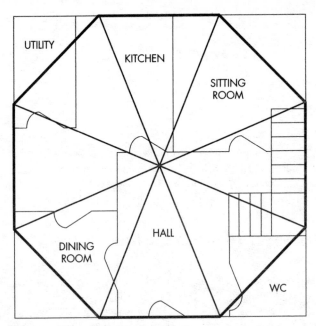

Figure 5.1   Overlaying the Pah Kwa on to the house plan

Missing sections

If your house is fairly square, you will find that the Pah Kwa sits comfortably on it. But if it's L-shaped, or T-shaped, or has a chunk out of one side, you may find that when you lay the Pah Kwa on the house plan there is an enrichment, or perhaps more than one, which doesn't have any part of your house within it.

These missing sections indicate an aspect of your life which is missing or diminished in some way. For example, if your house contains no children and family enrichment, you probably have no children, or those you have are out of touch or living away from home. If you have no health and happiness enrichment, you probably suffer poor health. A missing relationship enrichment suggests you have no permanent relationship – either you are single or you have short-term relationships only.

Ideally, all eight enrichments should be roughly in balance; each should be about the same size. But unless your house is square, they won't be in balance. A rectangular house will stretch the Pah Kwa shape when you overlay it, so that some enrichments are much larger than others. You will need to use feng shui to counter this imbalance.

You can, as always, remedy this; that's what feng shui is all about. The way to do it is to fill in the missing section of your house. This might sound impossible, but it is actually straightforward. Sometimes you can build on to the house, if you have the money and the space. You could add a conservatory to fill in the missing piece of an L-shaped house, or add an extension to fill in the space. But if this isn't possible, you can give the appearance that the missing piece is there by placing a mirror at the point where the missing section should begin (see Figure 5.2).

You can also use this technique to enlarge an enrichment which is too small. Suppose you are unhappy with your social life, and you have only a small section of your house within the friends and new beginnings enrichment. Place a mirror at a point where it will enlarge the friends and new beginnings enrichment, and you should find your social life improves as a result.

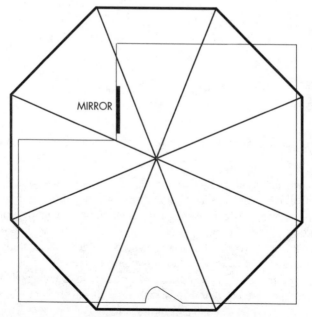

MIRROR

Figure 5.2 Position a mirror to create a missing section or enlarge one that is too small

Extra sections

Rather than have missing sections, some houses have extra sections (and some have both). If your house is rectangular, you will need to stretch the Pah Kwa in two directions to fit on top of the plan (see Figure 5.3). This means that the enrichments which are extended are much larger than the others.

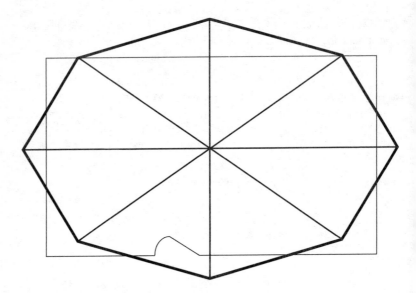

Figure 5.3 Stretching the Pah Kwa to fit over a rectangular house

If an enrichment is particularly large, this means that you have an abundance of it. This may be a good thing, or it may not – only you can know. A large friends and new beginnings enrichment might be more than you can cope with – perhaps your social life is too demanding and you seem to attract an awful lot of friends whom you don't particularly want. In this case, you will need to do something to reduce the size of this section of your house. On the other hand, you may love having a big circle of friends and be more than happy with your social life – in which case don't change anything in this part of the house.

If you decide to reduce the influence of an enrichment, you should make this part of the house less dominant. Reduce the light levels, keep doors closed to prevent the ch'i circulating too much, or perhaps use straight-line remedies to discourage the ch'i from becoming too expansive. You may also be able to use this part of the house less, by swapping round the rooms you use. If your dining room is in this enrichment, for example, could you put a table in the kitchen and eat there more often, and save the dining room for special occasions only?

Building an extension

If you add on an extension to your house, you will affect its feng shui. Either you will fill in a missing enrichment or you will add an extra section on to one of the enrichments. Before you do this, you should draw up a plan of how your house is going to look with the new extension, and then lay the Pah Kwa on to it (see Figure 5.4). Work out where all the enrichments fall – it may affect the enrichments which other parts of the house fall into – and make sure you are happy with this layout before you go ahead and build.

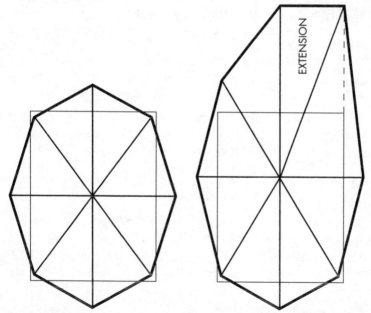

Figure 5.4 A new extension can change the enrichments into which other parts of the house fall

Upstairs and downstairs

The Pah Kwa overlays all the floors of your house in the same way, so that any upstairs room will fall in the same enrichment as the room beneath it. But suppose you have a larger ground floor than first floor if, for example, you have a single-storey kitchen extension? You might even have a larger upstairs. Some terraced houses have a section upstairs which protrudes into their neighbour's property.

If there is a section on one floor which is missing on another floor, you should rectify this. Either enlarge the missing section or reduce the extra section in the ways we have just looked at, in order to keep all the floors of the house in balance.

If your house has more than one storey, each one represents a slightly different aspect of yourself. The ground floor is yang, and represents the more open, obvious side of you which other people see and recognise. The first floor is more closely related to the private you – the side of you which only you, and perhaps your closest family and friends, tend to see.

So the ground floor pleasure and indulgence enrichment has a particularly strong influence on those pleasures which are public – partying, entertaining, eating out, playing bridge, playing tennis, and whatever else you choose to do for fun which involves other people. The upstairs pleasure and indulgence enrichment has more to do with private or secret pleasures – reading peacefully, having sex, eating secret bars of chocolate, or whatever else turns you on when you're alone (or almost alone).

If your house has more than two floors, each succeeding floor (going upwards) reflects a deeper and more private part of you. The second floor is concerned with the deeper intuitive aspects of your nature, and the attics will conceal the innermost part of you. If they are full of clutter and you never go into them, this indicates that you are not paying attention to the deeper and more spiritual aspects of yourself.

If you live in a flat or apartment, you should consider only those floors which you use. If your entrance is on the fifth floor, that is *your* first floor. (However, if you personally occupy an entire tower block, you will have a seriously multi-layered personality.)

General design

There are certain features which crop up in every room of the house, or almost every room, so we'll look at these first before we go through the house room by room. These features should be considered, whichever enrichment they fall into.

Windows and doors

Windows and doors are the entrances and exits to each room for the ch'i, so it is important that they should help it to flow in and out smoothly.

Windows

Windows should open outwards if possible, so the ch'i can get out as well as in. If the window faces west, it will let in unpredictable, often dangerous ch'i from the direction of the White Tiger. So these windows, especially, should never open inwards; it would be better not to open them at all.

Sash windows always block at least half of the window opening, even when they are fully open. If you cannot change the windows, you can encourage the ch'i in and out through the open half of the window by opening the lower part and placing a life or movement remedy on the window sill – a plant, perhaps, or an ornament which has movement, such as a Newton's cradle.

The shape of your windows is important because of the way it influences the ch'i as it enters. Square or roughly square windows are fine, but tall thin windows are harder for the ch'i to enter through. Ch'i loves round, octagonal and arched windows, but Gothic-style windows, which come to a point at the top, can be disruptive. You may get away with them if they face north, where they will wake up the sleepy Tortoise, but if they face west you will be provoking the already dangerous Tiger: don't take the risk. The Chinese often paint west-facing windows black to keep the Tiger out.

If you can't see out of the window clearly, the ch'i can't enter and leave easily. So avoid frosted glass unless you are trying to slow down ch'i, for example from the west. If the top of the window is too low to see through when you are standing up, this can cause depression, so make sure windows are set high enough.

An old house has its own character and personality, just as an old rock or tree does, and it is bad feng shui to damage it in any way. So you should never replace old windows with new ones (apart from repairing rotten windows with exact replicas). If your house has windows which open inwards, or are too small, or have Gothic arches to them, find remedies which don't involve tampering with the house's character. Use mirrors to encourage ch'i, wind chimes to slow it down, and rounded pelmets in front of pointed windows to smooth the flow of the ch'i.

Important points about windows

- Windows should open outwards, especially if they face west.
- Sash windows should be opened at the bottom and a life or movement remedy placed on the sill.
- Round, arched or octagonal windows are excellent, but windows which come to a point at the top are not good.
- The top of each window should be at eye level or above.
- Don't tamper with original windows in a period house.
- Windows should be kept clean and any damage, such as broken panes, should be repaired promptly. Make sure all your windows open and close easily and smoothly.

Doors

The most important door is the front door, which we'll consider in a moment, but all the other doors in the house are important, too. Enter each room in the house in turn and notice how you go through the door – the ch'i has to go the same way as you. Do you have to pull the door towards you in order to enter the room, or can you simply push it into the room? Are you greeted by a blank wall as you open the door, or does it open to give you a view of the whole room? Is your entrance blocked by a piece of furniture?

The door should be in proportion to the room. If it is too small, place a mirror inside the room to help the ch'i in; if it is too big, a wind chime will help to slow down the ch'i rushing out of it.

Important points about doors

- Doors should open into the room.
- They should not open on to a solid wall or the ch'i will be blocked, along with the part of your life governed by that enrichment.

■ There should not be any furniture blocking easy access into the room.

■ The door should be in proportion to the room.

■ Doors should always be kept clean and should move freely. If they jam, catch or don't close properly, remedy this straight away.

Your front door

The main link between the inside and the outside of your house is the front door. This is the main route in and out of the house not only for you, but also for the ch'i. So it's important that it should be right.

In order to make sure the front door is right, you have to consider what is outside it (we looked at this in Chapter 4). The ch'i arrives at the front door via whatever is outside it, and you need to think about whether this needs remedying. If there is too great a flow of ch'i – a long, straight, open path pointing at the door, for example – you will want to slow it down. But if the door is in a dark, overgrown area where the ch'i is inclined to stagnate, you need to speed it up. If you live in a flat where the ch'i is rushing past your door and down a staircase, you need to encourage it to make a diversion and enter through your front door.

There are three key factors in the design of your front door which you can use to influence the ch'i:

■ colour

■ glass panelling

■ pattern of decoration.

One way to change the effect of your front door is to change its colour. We've already looked at the effects of different colours and where to use them; paint the door a suitable colour to speed up or slow down the ch'i.

You can also add glass panelling to a solid door – or add a fanlight over it – to let more ch'i through. Equally, you could block in a glass panel to slow the ch'i down. You can add large or small glass panels, and use frosted or stained glass to calm the ch'i. Simply add or remove the right amount of glass to achieve the effect you need.

The decoration on the door, if you have any, will also influence the flow of ch'i. A round window or a curvy design will help the ch'i to flow gently.

A pattern of straight lines – such as vertical planking – will speed up the ch'i since it is a straight-line remedy.

Think about the size of your front door. As with other doors, it should be in proportion to the front hall. If it is too small, position mirrors in the hall to make it appear larger. If it is too big, on the other hand, hang a wind chime just inside it to prevent the ch'i rushing in too fast.

As with everything else, the front door should be kept clean, the paint should be refreshed frequently, and any damage should be repaired promptly. Lights outside the door help to encourage ch'i, but make sure you always replace blown bulbs straight away. The area around the front door, inside and out, should be kept free of clutter.

Entering through a different door Some people tend to enter their house through the back door, or through a side door, instead of using the front door. If you fall into this category, what does it mean in terms of feng shui? It doesn't alter the direction the house faces, which tells you how to lay the Pah Kwa on to it. But it does make a lot of difference to which enrichment you enter through.

The front door always – by definition – falls in the fame enrichment, which governs your public face and how you appear to the world. By avoiding the front door you are avoiding this aspect of yourself and your life. You may be a private person, who sees your home as an escape and a refuge from the outside world. You are not making use of the interface between the outer world and the home world, which suggests that you like to keep your public and private lives separate.

So which enrichment are you entering through? Presumably through one in which you are very much at home. If the door you typically use is in the pleasure and indulgence enrichment, for example, it is likely that you entertain a lot and enjoy relaxing at home – you see your house as somewhere to enjoy yourself, rather than as a place full of chores or loneliness.

Or perhaps you use a door in the health and happiness enrichment. If this is the case you are probably health conscious. Perhaps you frequently diet, or make a point of eating healthy food. You probably take plenty of exercise, use vitamin supplements and have an interest in health matters generally. You are likely to have a complementary medical practitioner of some kind whom you often visit – an osteopath, acupuncturist, homoeopath or reflexologist.

Establish in which enrichment the door you normally use is. Whichever it is, you will find that it is in an area which is particularly important to you, and probably in a positive way.

Walls and ceilings

A large, smooth, blank wall is discouraging to ch'i; ch'i simply rushes straight past it. So make your walls interesting to slow the ch'i down by hanging pictures or displaying ornaments. If you need to liven up the ch'i, you could add a dado or picture rail, but since these are straight-line remedies you should avoid them in rooms where the ch'i is already lively, and especially in the west.

If you live in an old house which already has these period features in rooms where the ch'i doesn't need to be any more lively, you shouldn't damage the character of the house by removing the dado or picture rails. Instead, soften the effect of the straight lines with rounded and curvy ornaments – such as plates hung above the picture rail. You can also help by breaking the line of the rail; a sofa with a high, rounded back positioned against a wall with a dado rail, will come up above the dado and break the line.

A cornice around the top of the walls is excellent since it prevents the ch'i getting stuck in the corner between the walls and the ceiling. If you are adding the cornice, choose a design which has a curvy profile.

If you use patterned wallpaper on the walls, choose a subtle pattern or you will distract the ch'i away from the rest of the room. Patterns with curving or rounded shapes are better for feng shui than square or checked designs.

The height of the ceiling should be in proportion to the room. If it's too low, raise it visually by painting it a lighter colour than the walls. Conversely, if it is too high, paint it a darker colour than the walls.

If your ceilings slope, this is good for helping the ch'i to flow harmoniously. However, if the bottom of the slope finishes below eye level, don't spend much time below it. This is not the place to put a bed, a sofa or a desk. Use the space for storage, keeping books or displaying ornaments.

Beams

If you live in a house with exposed beams, you need to pay these special attention. They are straight lines which can funnel ch'i until it becomes dangerously accelerated; the Chinese avoid them, but in the West they are popular. There are three main action points for improving the feng shui of a beamed house.

■ **Tone down the colour contrast between the beams and the ceiling**. Black beams against a white ceiling draw the ch'i to the beams, which is what you want to avoid. Strip the beams of paint or stain so that they are a less strident, more natural colour. You can also paint the ceiling off-white or even, perhaps, a darker colour so the beams create less of a contrast. In some beamed houses you can paint the beams themselves without detracting from the character of the house – an old boathouse with a beamed wooden ceiling, for example, could be painted pale blue or off-white throughout.

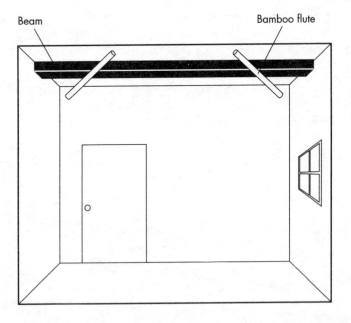

Figure 5.5   Break up the straight line of a beam by hanging bamboo flutes across it

■ **Break up the line of the beams**. Hang ribbons or wind chimes on the beams or, if you want a less oriental look, hang wicker baskets or old china jugs (but not dried flowers – anything dead is bad feng shui). You can also use a straight-line remedy, surprisingly; place bamboo flutes – or similar straight objects – across the beam at an angle of 45 degrees. Put a bamboo flute at each end of the beam, about a third of the way in from the wall. One end of the flute should point at the ceiling and the other at the wall. The effect of this is to cut across the corner where the wall and ceiling meet, and at the same time to create the top half of a Pah Kwa (see Figure 5.5).

■ **Avoid spending a lot of time beneath a beam**. Don't place any furniture which you spend a lot of time on, such as a bed or favourite chair, under a beam. You should also avoid positioning the cooker or sink under a beam, or any other piece of furniture or equipment which you use regularly.

Colour in the house

Different colours are suitable in different parts of the house, depending on which way the house faces and where the ch'i in that area is coming from. In the west of the house, for example, you would use different colours from those you would use in the east. In each part of the house, you should choose your palette according to whether you want to encourage or slow down the ch'i.

You should also take into account your own element – or the element of the person who most often uses the room. The colours which are appropriate to your element will always be suitable for a room which you use. If, for example, you are a strongly water person, you will probably be horrified at the thought of using bright purple, orange or red to liven up the ch'i in the south area of your house. However, you can use a bright blue (which is an enlivening water colour) instead.

If you need to liven up the ch'i with bright colours such as purple or yellow, this doesn't mean you have to paint all the walls in a garish purple. You could use a more neutral (but still lively) colour such as a yellowy ivory on the walls, and then use flashes of purple in cushions, rugs and curtains, and in the decoration. You might have a vase containing plum-coloured ostrich feathers, a pair of purple glass candlesticks, or a pile of cream, lilac, and purple hat boxes on top of a cupboard.

The following chart shows which element and which colours are appropriate for each direction. So, for example, fire is the element which is at home in the south. In south rooms, or in any part of the house predominantly used by a fire person (see Chapter 3 to establish your own element), reds, purples, oranges and yellows will strengthen ch'i. If you need to damp down the effects of the ch'i, you can use green.

Direction	Element	Colours to encourage ch'i	Colours to slow down ch'i
South or south-east	Fire	Purple, red, orange, yellow	Green
North	Water	Bright blue and black, or white and gold	Soft, muted blue
East or north-east	Wood	Green	Blue and black
West or north-west	Metal	Gold and white	Brown and earthy yellow such as ochre
South-west	Earth	Earthy brown and yellow	Soft deep red, lilac

Rooms and their feng shui

We've already established that the feng shui of each room is determined by various factors, such as the direction it faces and the enrichment in which it falls. But there are additional factors which are specific to each type of room, and we're going to look at these now.

The hall

The hall is the first room you enter when you come in through the front door, so it is also the room the ch'i first enters. It is critical that you invite the ch'i in, and then encourage it to circulate so that it can go on to reach all the rest of the house. A stagnating hall, one which is poky or dark, can have a damaging effect on the entire house by preventing the ch'i from flowing harmoniously before it has even begun.

We've already seen how the size of the hall and the front door should be in proportion to each other. If the door is too large, you can slow down the ch'i with a wind chime or banner hung just inside it. But generally, the hall should encourage the ch'i in. It isn't a place to sit and relax; it's a place for coming and going and bustle and activity, so you want a good lively flow of ch'i.

Remove any clutter from your hall. If you simply can't put it anywhere else, buy or build a cupboard to hide it in. Paint the hall a light, bright, welcoming colour, appropriate to the direction it faces. Hang a mirror to make it appear larger and brighter. If it is small, hang the mirror opposite the front door; if it is large, hang the mirror at right angles to the door. If the hall is long and thin, hang a mirror on one of the long walls.

Many front halls, especially in flats, don't have windows. In this case, you must make a special effort to brighten up the area and put a high wattage bulb in the light. If you do have a window, keep the curtains well drawn back during the day to let in the maximum light; make opening the curtains the first job you do when you come downstairs in the morning, and do it with a flourish to let in the light and the ch'i.

If the stairs dominate the hall, don't box them in but have open banisters so the ch'i can flow in and out. If the stairs face the door, there is a danger that the ch'i will run straight down them and out through the door, so you need to slow it down. If you have room, put a screen between the bottom of the stairs and the front door. Otherwise hang a wind chime or ribbon from the ceiling between the stairs and the front door.

Key points for good hall feng shui

- The hall should be light, bright and welcoming.
- It should be uncluttered.
- Use mirrors to make the hall appear larger and more in proportion.
- Divert any ch'i which is rushing down the stairs and out through the front door.
- Leave the doors which open off the hall open as often as you can so that the light comes in and the ch'i can flow easily all round the house.

Stairs

Ch'i travels up and down stairs just as we do, so it needs to be encouraged to do so freely and easily. Staircases should be as wide as possible, so keep them free from clutter and mess. Don't use them for storing shoes, books or anything else. Don't have a door at the top or bottom of the stairs or the ch'i will be unable to move to the next floor; if you already have such a door either remove it or leave it permanently open. Avoid open-tread stairs since these help the ch'i to flow down and around, but discourage it from flowing upwards.

Straight runs of stairs can speed the ch'i up too much, so slow it down with wind chimes hung above them. Stairs with a lot of twists and turns have the opposite effect – the ch'i stagnates – so help it down by hanging mirrors at the bends, or even by painting a flowing mural design on the wall for it to follow.

Key points for good stairs feng shui

- Staircases should be wide and clear of clutter.
- Avoid doors on staircases, and open-tread stairs.
- Slow down ch'i on a straight run of stairs using wind chimes above the stairs.
- Help ch'i down twisting stairs with mirrors or murals.

Corridors and landings

The wider and brighter your corridors and landings are, the better. Use mirrors to make them seem wider if necessary, and keep some of the doors which lead off them open to let in more light and give a greater feeling of space. Break up long, narrow corridors by hanging wind chimes, banners, or some other object which will slow down the ch'i, from the ceiling.

If a corridor is short you can lengthen it by hanging a mirror at one or both ends to open it up and help the ch'i to flow more smoothly along and around it. It will also help to open the doors which lead off it.

The way doors are aligned in corridors is important. If two opposite doors are not quite aligned, you should remedy this with a mirror beside each which reflects the section of the opposite door which projects out. If two opposite doors are of different sizes, the larger one should lead to the more important room. If this isn't the case, a mirror on the large door will reflect the smaller one and make it seem larger.

If a long corridor or landing has a door at the end, facing back down the corridor, the ch'i will be funnelled towards it. Hang wind chimes along the corridor and outside the door, or some other object which will slow down the ch'i.

Doors which open so that they hit each other are very bad feng shui, and will cause conflict in whatever enrichment they fall. Re-hang one of the doors to prevent this, or replace it with narrow double doors which don't reach as far as the other door.

Key points for good corridor and landing feng shui

- They should be wide and bright.
- Use mirrors to make them appear wider.
- Leave doors open to make the corridor or landing brighter.
- Break up long, narrow corridors with wind chimes or banners.
- Doors facing each other should be aligned; if they aren't, use mirrors to redress this.
- Don't allow doors to hit each other when they are open.

Kitchens

For many people, the kitchen is the most important room in the house – the heart of the home. If you can, site it in an enrichment which is suitable for you. If it is in your health and happiness enrichment, it will be an excellent place to cook good, healthy food. It is well suited to the wealth enrichment, too, because the Chinese words for food and wealth sound similar.

If the kitchen is in the pleasure and indulgence enrichment, you will find that you entertain in there a lot. In this position, and with a kitchen large enough to have a table you can eat at, you will probably find that an evening's entertaining starts and ends in the kitchen, and never goes near the sitting room. With this arrangement, you need not bother with a dining room – use the room for something else.

The kitchen should be light and bright, with no dark corners. If necessary, use mirrors or lights to brighten up any dead areas. You can also use light or reflective materials such as stainless steel for cookers and pale marble (if you can afford it) for work surfaces. At least you could have a marble slab sitting on a work surface, which is ideal for making pastry as well as for lightening up a dull area.

An untidy kitchen makes for bad feng shui, so make sure everything has its place and is regularly tidied away; at least, make yourself tidy up every night before you go to bed. Use vegetable baskets, spice shelves, racks inside cupboard doors, and anything else to enable you to keep food, spices, crockery and pots and pans off the work surfaces and out of the way.

One of the most important considerations in the kitchen is that when you are working in there, you should be able to see anyone entering or leaving the room. So try to avoid a layout which means you have your back to the door when you are at the sink, cooker or work surface. If you can't avoid this, at least you can place a mirror so that you can see the door reflected in it (see Figure 5.6).

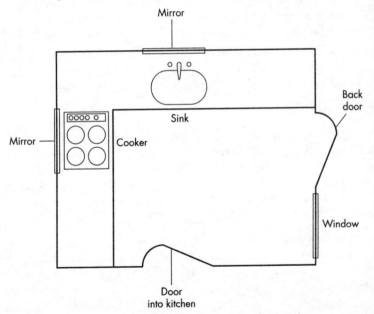

Figure 5.6 A poor kitchen layout, remedied using mirrors

In an ideal layout, the cooker and the sink should not be next to each other, since they represent the elements of fire and water, which don't combine well (see Figure 5.7). Separate them as far as possible, and place a wooden object between the two of them, such as a chopping board or a wicker vegetable basket. You can site the refrigerator facing the door because you spend very little time at it, so your back will rarely face the door directly.

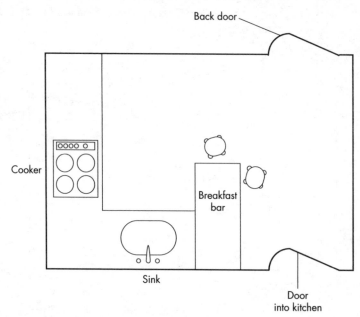

Figure 5.7   A good kitchen layout

Often a kitchen has two doors, one leading to the hall or another room and the other leading outside. If people tend to use the kitchen to pass straight through without stopping, so will the ch'i. So slow it down by creating a diversion. If the room is large enough, place a table in the middle so that it is necessary to weave round it in order to cross the kitchen from door to door (see Figure 5.8).

Key points for good kitchen feng shui

- Site the kitchen in a suitable enrichment for you.
- Make sure the room is light and bright, with no dark corners.
- Keep the room tidy.
- Position mirrors so that you can see the door when you are cooking or washing up.

■ Separate the cooker and the sink, with a wooden object between the two.

■ If the kitchen has two doors which turn it into a corridor, impede the direct route from one to the other.

■ All kitchen equipment, cookers and fridges should be kept clean and in working order.

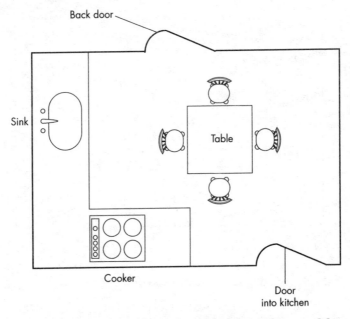

Figure 5.8 A strategically placed kitchen table will slow the ch'i down if the kitchen is used as a corridor

Sitting rooms

Think about which enrichment this room falls in. Is it a suitable one such as pleasure and indulgence or friends and new beginnings? If you spend most of your rest time with your children (if this isn't a contradiction in terms), a sitting room in the children and family enrichment would be suitable. If you spend a lot of time alone and like to sit and read, the wisdom enrichment might be good for your sitting room.

If your sitting room is not in the enrichment you would like it to be, and you can't swap your rooms around, introduce a remedy which would suit the enrichment you would like for your sitting room. For example, if you would like it to be in your friends and new beginnings enrichment, choose remedies which suit this enrichment. Sound remedies are the best for your friends and new beginnings enrichment, so put a chiming clock or a CD player in the sitting room to represent the friends and new beginnings enrichment.

Below is a reminder of the eight enrichments and the remedies which suit each one.

Enrichment	Remedy
Fame	Light
Health and happiness	Straight lines
Pleasure and indulgence	Stillness
Friends and new beginnings	Sound
Relationship	Movement
Children and family	Colour
Wisdom and experience	Mechanical device
Wealth	Life

As always, make sure this room is bright and has no dead corners or alcoves. As well as using colour and light to lift these areas, you can also place a pot plant as a life remedy – but make sure it has rounded, not spiky, leaves. You can also use plants to soften sharp corners jutting into the room, which could aggravate the ch'i. Either place a tall plant in front of the corner, or attach a shelf higher up and train a trailing plant to cover the corner.

The layout of the seating in the sitting room is the most important aspect of the room. You should aim for the seating to create something as close to a circle, octagon or square as you can manage. It's likely that at least one wall will be taken up with a fireplace (the traditional focal point of the sitting room) or a television (the modern-day focus). The remaining seats should be arranged to avoid creating a line-up or corridor of chairs and sofas (see Figure 5.9).

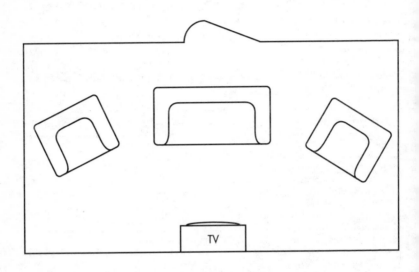

Figure 5.9 A poor sitting-room layout where the seating creates a corridor

The sitting room should not be cluttered with furniture, or the ch'i cannot flow around it. So make sure the amount of furniture, and its size, suits the proportions of the room. A mirror in the room, preferably above the fireplace, will help to create a feeling of space (see Figure 5.10).

There is one seat in the room, or occasionally more than one, which is known by the Chinese as 'honoured guest' position. This is the best seat in the room and you can tell which one it is because everyone always wants to sit there. It is always comfortable and it faces the door so that its occupant is in control of who enters and leaves the room. You can't spring any surprises on the person in honoured guest position.

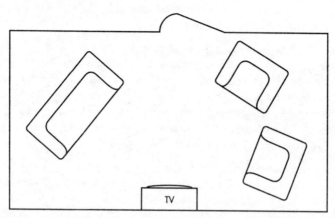

Figure 5.10 Seating should be arranged around four sides, or three if the fourth side accommodates the fireplace or television

Key points for good sitting room feng shui

■ Choose a suitable enrichment for your sitting room, or introduce the appropriate remedy for the enrichment in which you would like the room to fall.

■ Keep the sitting room light and bright, using colour, light and pot plants to remedy dark or sharp corners.

■ Arrange the furniture to create a circle, square or octagon of seats, and avoid cluttering the room with too much furniture.

■ Make sure you have an honoured guest position opposite the door.

■ The room should be warm and cosy, with pictures and ornaments, but it should not be cluttered with children's toys or piles of old magazines.

Dining rooms

As with the kitchen and sitting rooms, find a suitable enrichment for this room if you can, or incorporate a remedy which suits the enrichment you would have chosen if you could.

Arrange the furniture so that the focus is on the table, and the food when it is spread out on it. The table should be oval or round if possible; square tables are acceptable but long, thin tables funnel the ch'i and create an atmosphere in which it is difficult to relax.

Make sure there is plenty of room to open the door and walk around the table and chairs without feeling cramped. If you can't do this you need a smaller table. If this means you haven't room for all the friends you like to entertain, don't cram them into an over-full room or they'll all end up with indigestion. Change your arrangements so that you eat buffet style, or in the kitchen. Mirrors will help the room to feel larger; they should be placed so they reflect the food on the table.

If the dining room is too close to the front door, people won't stay long after they've eaten. If you can't change the layout, at least keep the dining room door closed once the food is served.

The kitchen is a very yang area, and eating in here is not necessarily relaxing. However, if what you want is stimulating conversation over meals, this may not matter to you. You can also relax better in the kitchen if it is in the pleasure and indulgence enrichment. If you do like to entertain in the kitchen, create a more yin feel to it by lowering the lighting once the food is served. Either put the lights on a dimmer switch, or turn off the main light and use only table lights.

Key points for good dining room feng shui

- Find the most suitable enrichment you can for the dining room.
- Focus on the table, which should be round, oval or octagonal.
- Don't overcrowd the room with furniture.
- Don't locate the dining room in sight of the front door.
- If you eat in the kitchen, reduce the lighting once the meal is served.

Utility rooms

These rooms are full of energy, with machines buzzing and whirring and clanking, and stirring up the ch'i. If you possibly can, locate this room in the east of the house, where the gentle ch'i from the Green Dragon will be able to cope. Or locate the room in the wisdom and experience enrichment, traditionally governed by the Green Dragon, where mechanical devices are most at home.

Even so, wherever you site the room, you need to keep it as calm as possible to counteract all that frenetic energy. The bigger the room, the more scope there is for the ch'i to circulate and dissipate the energy. Use a restful colour in this room; paint it a soft blue or green, or a pastel shade, to suit its direction.

Try to avoid lining up the machines opposite or alongside each other; stagger them as much as possible. A clothes airer down the centre of a long room, or across a wider one, will help to slow down the ch'i as it has to negotiate all the damp clothes (see Figure 5.11). However, a clothes airer creates a straight line, so soften this by hanging the clothes irregularly across and along it when you can, rather than accentuating the lines with clothes hung in regimented rows.

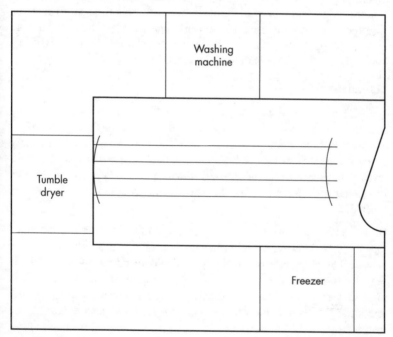

Figure 5.11 The machines in this utility room are placed to spread their energy around the room, and the clothes on the airer help to slow down the ch'i further

Bathrooms

You should always be able to see the door from the bath, shower, lavatory or basin. If you can't, place a mirror in a position where it reflects the door. The room should be as uncluttered as possible, so make sure you have plenty of cupboards and shelves on which to store everything.

A bathroom is used to invigorate and refresh, but also to relax and wind down, make sure you can do both in your bathroom. Decorate it in bright, fresh, clean colours, but place low lighting or candles so that you can turn the main light off and relax if you need to.

It is bad feng shui for the first view when you open the door to be of the lavatory. If you can't move the lavatory, screen it off, perhaps with a towel rail protruding from the wall. Sometimes, re-hanging the door to hinge on the other side does the trick. If you can't manage this either, hang a wind chime just inside the door as a distraction. The bathroom door should be kept closed when the room is not being used.

Lavatories

If you leave the lavatory seat up, the ch'i will be flushed away along with the water. Water is associated with wealth, so you will flush your money away every time you flush the lavatory. This applies even more strongly if the lavatory is in your wealth enrichment. Otherwise, you also flush away your pleasure and indulgence, friends and new beginnings, wisdom or whatever is governed by the enrichment in which the lavatory is located.

If you have a lavatory which is separate from the bathroom, it shouldn't face the door. However, this is often unavoidable. In this case, you want a window above the lavatory, which you should keep bright and inviting. If the view is good, make it easy to see (people can always draw the curtains once they're in the room). If the view is poor, put a pot plant on the windowsill. If there is no window above the lavatory, hang a mirror there instead.

Bedrooms

It's vital to get the feng shui of your bedroom right; after all, you spend more time there than anywhere else. Do your best to make sure your bedroom falls in an enrichment which is right for you – ideally, pleasure and indulgence, relationship or health and happiness. If it doesn't, swap with another room if you possibly can. Otherwise, bring in remedies which suit the enrichment you would like your bedroom to be in.

It is also a good idea to have a bedroom which faces in the direction which suits your personal element:

- Fire: south or south-east
- Water: north
- Wood: east or north-east
- Metal: west or north-west
- Earth: south-west.

If you can't manage to get your bedroom into the right enrichment or facing the right way, there is one more thing you should be able to manage. Lay the Pah Kwa over your bedroom only, with the fame enrichment over the direction the room faces, and see which part of the room to put the bed in – either a suitable enrichment within the room, or in the direction which suits your own element. If you're not sure which way the room faces, use your intuition. Most rooms face the window, but sometimes you sense that a room faces the door, especially if there are no windows, or the windows are very small, or if the door is particularly large.

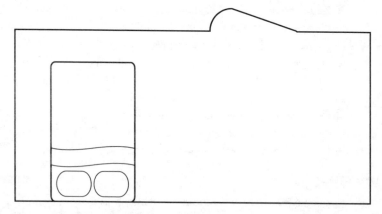

Figure 5.12 This is a suitable arrangement for a bedroom, in which the bed does not face the door directly, but has a clear view of it

Position the bed so that you can easily see people entering and leaving through the door (see Figure 5.12). Don't point the foot of the bed directly at the door: dead people are laid out like that before being carried out feet first. If you can't see the door easily from the bed – and you can't reposition the bed – hang a mirror so the door is reflected in it when you lie in bed.

The bed should not sit directly underneath a light, as this is bad feng shui. The energy from the light, even when it is off, is disruptive when you are trying to sleep. If you can't change this arrangement, at least make sure the light is never used, and use a side light instead.

The bed itself needs the ch'i to flow over, around and under it. This means that a bed which sits on the floor with no space under it is bad feng shui as it prevents the ch'i from flowing beneath it. Use a bed in the old-fashioned style which sits well clear of the floor. You should use a headboard, even if it is simply attached to the wall and not to the bed at all. Choose one which suits your personal element:

- Fire: angular in shape and in a bright colour
- Water: a curvy shape and coloured blue or green
- Wood: squared and wooden
- Metal: steel, iron or brass
- Earth: use natural rather than synthetic materials in natural, unbleached and undyed colours.

Key points for good bedroom feng shui

- Do your best to get the bedroom in the most beneficial enrichment for you.
- Place the bed so you can see the door from it.
- Don't position the bed underneath a light fitting.
- Use a bed which sits well above the floor.
- Choose a headboard which suits your personal element.

The study

Many homes have a study, whether they double up as a spare room or a dining room, or are a dedicated work place in their own right. Clearly, the enrichment in which the study falls is important; if it is in the pleasure and indulgence enrichment you won't get much work done, although it might be an ideal room to use for a hobby. If you are a keen gardener and have a study for your gardening books, to do your planning and to work out your bulb catalogue orders, this might be the perfect place for it. However, if you use it to pay bills or to earn money, or to learn or study, find a more suitable enrichment such as wealth or wisdom and experience if you can.

If you use your study to earn money, don't place it near the front door where the money can run out, or facing the top of the stairs where it will run down the stairs. If you really can't move it, keep the door shut especially when you're working.

Often, a study is part of another room such as a sitting room or bedroom. This is fine, but try to choose a room in a suitable enrichment. In any case lay the Pah Kwa on to the room alone and work out which is the wealth or wisdom and experience enrichment within the room and place the desk there. As we saw before, you'll need to establish which way the room faces. Most face the window, but you can sense that some rooms face the door if it is much more dominant than the window.

Balance the two uses of the room, in terms of both space and lighting. Don't cram a tiny study into the corner of a large dining room, or into the tiny space under the hall stairs. Cramped studies don't give your wealth or your intellect room to expand. Make sure that a well-lit study area is balanced by good lighting in the rest of the room.

The desk itself is important. You shouldn't sit with your back to a door; if you can't avoid it, hang a mirror above the desk. However short of space you are, have the largest desk you can manage; you don't want to be cramped. Always keep the desk tidy and free from clutter.

Key points for good study feng shui

- Find a suitable enrichment if possible, such as wealth or wisdom and experience.
- Avoid having a study near the front door or facing the top of the stairs.
- If the study doubles with another room, find a room in a suitable enrichment, and place the desk in the best enrichment within the room. Balance the two functions within the room.
- Don't sit with your back to the door.
- Have a spacious and clear working area on your desk.

Creating good feng shui in your home isn't difficult; it just requires thought and a methodical approach. If you feel your house needs a huge amount of work, simply tackle one area at a time, starting with the enrichments you feel are most important, and work through the house a stage at a time. Or you could tackle the new beginnings enrichment first, to help get you started. Before you've finished, you'll already have started to feel the benefits of the first changes – and that will give you the encouragement you need to keep going.

6 | FENG SHUI IN THE GARDEN

The Chinese first identified the influence of the landscape and surroundings on their lives by studying outdoor locations – burial sites, in fact. So the outdoor world is an obvious place to practise the art of feng shui today. Good feng shui in the garden will improve your health and success in life – and it will improve your garden, too.

The Pah Kwa and your garden

You need to study the feng shui of your garden separately from the feng shui of your house, which means you have to overlay the Pah Kwa on to a garden plan. In order to do this you need to know whether to treat all the sections of garden (if you have more than one) together or independently.

How many gardens?

Suppose you have a front garden and a back garden. Or a garden which runs along two sides of the house. Or you may have an alleyway linking the front and back, or a vegetable garden leading off the main garden. Should you work out the feng shui for each separately, or should they all be treated as parts of one garden?

There isn't an exact answer to this; feng shui is an intuitive art at times – and this is one of those times. The key factor is whether you regard the various parts of your garden as one or more. If your front and back gardens are completely separate, or have only a short passageway linking them, treat them separately and feng shui each of them. If the house is in the middle of a plot with garden all around (which the Chinese consider the perfect arrangement), feng shui the whole lot together.

Most gardens, however, aren't this accommodating. They are, for example, mostly at the back of the house but there may be a narrow strip running along the side which is wider than just an alley, but not exactly proper garden. You have to use your own judgement in these gardens. If you feel the two (or more) sections are really all one, feng shui them accordingly, and treat them as such when you come to work on the design. However, if you think of them as separate gardens, feng shui them separately.

The way in which you regard these borderline gardens can say as much about you as it does about the garden. If you instinctively view the front and back gardens separately, even though they are linked, it suggests that you like to keep these two parts of your life separate. Someone else might look at the same garden differently because they are the kind of person who likes their life to be more integrated.

If you treat your front and back gardens separately, think of the front garden as yang and the back garden as yin. In the ideal south-facing house, this is exactly how it would be. The front garden would be in the yang south direction and the back garden in the yin north direction. Even if you aren't lucky enough to live in a south-facing house, you should still think of the front garden as the open, expansive, public yang area, facing the world, and the back garden as the nurturing, private, quiet, yin area.

So make your front garden as light and open as you can, letting in ch'i from the south especially by removing or lowering any high hedges or fences on this side. Think in terms of creating a more private feel in the back garden, with plenty of light but with the ch'i encouraged from the north to give the garden a relaxed feel.

Working out the direction of your garden

In order to lay the Pah Kwa over your garden – or each of your gardens – you will need to establish which way the garden faces. Then, as with the house, you can lay the fame enrichment in this direction, and read the rest of the enrichments off from there.

Most gardens are considered to face the door or gate through which they are usually entered. In the case of the back garden, this is typically the back door of the house. However, if you have more than one back door, or usually enter through a side gate, you should assume that the garden faces towards the most frequently used entrance.

The front garden, of course, has at least two entrances – one from the house and one from the road or public area beyond the garden. Since the front garden is a yang area, it is your public face to the outside world; the first area that visitors to the house see. So it is considered to face out from the house towards the road. If you are treating your entire garden plot, with or without the house, as one complete area, you should lay the fame enrichment over the front gate which leads to the world beyond.

There are exceptions to these guidelines, however, and this is where your intuition takes over. Some gardens – particularly back gardens – don't follow this pattern; you can feel it. If you can sense that this description of the garden direction is wrong, it probably is. If you stand in your back garden and find yourself feeling that it really doesn't face the back door, go with your instincts.

The gardens which most often face in some other direction are those with wide views away from the house. To give you an obvious example, suppose you have a house on an open cliff-top. The back garden occupies the area between the house and the cliff edge. If you decided that the garden faced the house, that would put its back to the cliff. You can probably sense that this feels wrong just from reading it here – you don't even need to see the garden. In this case, the garden would face the broad, wide view across the sea.

Where does the house fit in?

The separate house and garden, each with their own Pah Kwa, represent the inner and outer aspects of your life. The feng shui of your house is to do with your personal and private attitudes, feelings and behaviour. The garden represents the things outside and around you, the people and influences which affect you. For example, the wealth enrichment of your garden will be concerned with the outer aspects of the money you earn: your employer's judgement (or otherwise) regarding whether to increase it, or other people's decisions about whether to offer you more lucrative work. The wealth enrichment of the house complements this by governing your own attitude to money: how you spend or save it, whether you choose to ask for a raise, whether you are prone to debt or to stinginess, and so on.

Equally, the relationship enrichment of your garden influences how your partner (or prospective partner) sees you, and their attitude towards you. The relationship enrichment of the house, on the other hand, is more concerned with your attitude to your partner, how you cope with the relationship, which areas of it you find most stressful and most pleasurable, and so on. So the house is you and the garden is the world immediately around you.

If you have a house and garden which are more suited to being treated as one unit for feng shui purposes, this indicates a more integrated approach to your life. You have been drawn to this kind of house and garden because you need – and perhaps already have – a more integrated lifestyle. In this case, you will overlay the octagonal Pah Kwa on to the whole plot. Some enrichments will be occupied by the house, others by the garden.

The enrichments which fall only within the house are likely to be more private aspects of your life. If the relationship enrichment is within the house, perhaps you keep your relationships very separate from work, or you don't introduce your partners to friends or family, or maybe you have affairs. If the wealth enrichment is within the house, maybe you earn your money in private, working alone, or perhaps you have a private income.

By the way, if you treat the house and garden as one unit, you can still feng shui the house on its own, as we saw in Chapter 5. You can lay the Pah Kwa on to any plan, large or small, to find its own areas of enrichment. You can feng shui an individual room to find the most appropriate enrichments in which to place each piece of furniture. You can even feng shui your kitchen work surface, or your desk, or even a window box.

Missing and enlarged sections

The same thing applies here as applies to missing and enlarged sections of the house, which we looked at in Chapter 5. If your garden or plot is not 'square', you will find that certain enrichments within the Pah Kwa do not sit over the garden at all, or that there are sections of garden protruding beyond the edge of the Pah Kwa. An L-shaped garden will be missing a chunk; a garden with an extra section tagged on at one corner will stick out beyond the Pah Kwa.

Again, as we saw with the house, a missing section indicates that that enrichment is missing or reduced in your life. If you have no children, you may find the children and family enrichment isn't there; if you never have much money, the wealth section may be missing, and so on.

Extra sections indicate areas where you are well blessed, although you may feel too well blessed. If you have a lot of children, you may find you have an enlarged children and family enrichment. An enlarged fame section suggests that you are successful at work or highly respected – a local councillor, perhaps, or on the board of governors of the local school.

Matching the garden to its enrichments

The next stage in applying feng shui to your garden is to look at what you use each section of the garden for. You need to suit each activity to the best enrichment you can. For instance, do you have a barbecue? Which enrichment is it in? If it is in your wealth enrichment, you are burning money every time you light it. It would be much better to put it in the pleasure and indulgence section, or in the friends and new beginnings enrichment if you usually light it when you are entertaining. It is also suited to the south or south-east of the garden, since these are the directions of the fire element.

What about the children's swings or sandpit? Try to put these in the children and family enrichment. Grow herbs in the health and happiness enrichment, and so on. Below is an idea of the types of activities and features which suit each enrichment of the garden.

- **Fame.** This is the area for building your reputation, so use it to entertain people you are trying to impress. You could also use it for growing giant vegetables or prize plants which you want to show off. Don't try to do anything private here as you're likely to be disturbed; it's not the place for a quiet seat for meditating or reading.
- **Health and happiness**. Have your quiet seat for resting and relaxing here, perhaps near to the sound of water. This is also the place to grow herbs for healing and for fresh, healthy cooking. You might want a vegetable garden here, too.
- **Pleasure and indulgence.** Have your best fun in this part of the garden. This is a good spot for the barbecue and for a table and chairs. Or you could put a swimming pool here. If you enjoy more private pursuits, this is the spot for your dream garden if you're a gardener – the one you really want to spend lots of time tending.
- **Friends and new beginnings.** This is another good area for the barbecue, or for seating. Or if you and your friends are

more active, put up the badminton set here. It's also a good spot for a greenhouse or a seed bed, where you propagate new plants. You can also keep your dustbins here to symbolise a continual throwing out of the old to make way for the new.

■ **Relationship.** What do you and your partner enjoy doing together in the garden? Whatever it is, this is the place to do it. So put a romantic seat here under a bower, or the greenhouse if you like to work in the greenhouse together. This is the place for activities you share with your partner. If you are single and would like a relationship, keep this area tidy and free from weeds. Plant perennial rather than annual flowers and a fruit tree which will blossom and bear fruit.

■ **Children and family**. If you have children, grandchildren, or frequent visitors with children, this is the place to make safe for them. Don't grow any poisonous or thorny plants here, and make sure fences and boundaries are safe and secure. This is the area for a sandpit, a swing, a tree-house or a paddling pool.

■ **Wisdom and experience**. Use this part of the garden to learn and grow. Grow new plants here in trial beds, or have a private seat where you sit and read or meditate. This is also the best place to put the compost heap, where it can mature and grow into a rich mulch for your other plants.

■ **Wealth**. This means material possessions as well as money, so use this area to store things which aren't just junk. You could keep your garden shed here, and store garden furniture in the winter. If you make money from your garden, for example by selling vegetables or chutneys and jams, this is the place to grow the produce if you can.

Obviously, you won't be able to do all of these things in every garden. Some enrichments may be missing, and you may have to find a second or third choice of enrichment for some activities. It's all very well advising you to grow produce for selling in the wealth enrichment, and if you can you should, but if you make tomato chutney and your wealth enrichment faces north, it's not going to be a great place to grow tomatoes. So follow these guidelines as closely as you can, but don't be devastated if it doesn't work out perfectly; a second choice of enrichment, and often a third, will usually be fine.

Using remedies in the garden

As we saw in Chapter 5, if you can't find a suitable enrichment for a particular activity, you can represent the enrichment you would have chosen by bringing in a suitable remedy. If you have no children and family area but want a swing for your grandchildren when they visit, site it in the best enrichment you can find, such as health and happiness. Then bring into that enrichment a colour remedy, which is the type of remedy best suited to the children and family enrichment. In this instance, you could simply buy (or paint) a brightly coloured swing.

There are eight types of remedy you can use, as we saw in Chapter 4. Each one is particularly suited to one of the eight enrichments. Each one is also related to one of the eight compass directions. Suppose you want a remedy in your wisdom and experience area which falls, say, in the south. Should you use a functional device (the remedy for the enrichment) or light (the remedy for the direction)? The answer is that you can use either, but you should try to combine both. In this example you could use an outdoor light, which is both a device and a light remedy. Or use two remedies, one of each type, such as a garden tap (a functional device) and a mirror (for light).

Below is a table reminder of the eight remedies, and for which enrichment and direction each is best suited. As you will realise, if your garden faces south the same remedy will suit both the direction and the enrichment for each part of the garden, since they will align: fame will be in the south, health and happiness in the south-west and so on. If your garden faces any other way, read off both the remedy for the enrichment and the remedy for the direction, for the part of the garden in question.

Remedy	Enrichment	Direction
Light	Fame	South
Straight lines	Health and happiness	South-west
Stillness	Pleasure and indulgence	West
Sound	Friends and family	North-west
Movement	Relationship	North
Colour	Children and family	North-east
Functional device	Wisdom and experience	East
Life	Wealth	South-east

Let's take a look at each of the eight remedies in turn, and see what kind of garden objects and features you can use as remedies, and where you might use them.

- **Light**. Ch'i does not readily venture into dark areas, so you need to encourage it. A balance of light and shade is a good thing, and ch'i likes some shade in a garden, but there is a difference between shade and a dark, overgrown, impenetrable corner. You can bring light to an area with garden lights, of course, or with a mirror. You can also introduce water which reflects light into the area, especially if it is moving. You can increase the light by pruning and cutting back overgrown plants and trees.

- **Straight lines**. If ch'i is too inclined to stagnate, perhaps in the sleepy north, or in an area of the garden with a lot of large shrubs, you can speed it up with straight lines. These can be either horizontal or vertical. A straight path forms an excellent remedy, as does a wooden bench with a slatted seat. Vertical straight lines include arches – especially arches with an angular or straight design – and obelisks, as well as tall, straight plants such as bamboo or foxgloves. A straight, vertical water jet makes a good vertical straight line, and a single straight water channel through part of the garden is a perfect horizontal remedy.

- **Stillness**. Slow down over-active ch'i with a large, still object such as a simple, solid statue, or a large urn or pot. Or you could use a still pool in a simple shape, such as a circle. This kind of remedy is particularly useful in the west, where it helps to calm down the potentially dangerous White Tiger ch'i.

- **Sound.** You can introduce noise to the garden in all sorts of ways to help wake up sleepy ch'i. Some plants make noises, such as quivering aspen trees, or euphorbias with seed pods which pop. You can also hang wind chimes, or install a fountain or waterfall to create a gentle sound. If you feed the birds in this part of the garden it is likely to become noisier, too. Or you can fill this part of the garden with children's toys and children to play with them.

- **Movement**. Feeding the birds is a good idea for this kind of remedy as well as for a sound remedy. You can also use a water feature in which the water moves, such as a stream or a spout on the wall which spills water into a pool. Plants which move easily in the breeze, such as tall ornamental grasses, also help to bring movement to the area and enliven ch'i which is sleepy or stagnant.

- **Colour**. Colour can be used to slow down or speed up ch'i. You should also match the colour of flowers, leaves and berries to the right part of the garden – fire colours in the south and so on (which we'll look at later). If the part of the garden you are considering is in balance, use the colours which match its direction, but if it needs remedying, use different colours to speed up or slow down the ch'i. Calm greens, blues, whites and pastels will help to calm ch'i, while bright colours will wake it up. You don't have to add colour through plants; you can introduce painted furniture or ornaments, or brightly coloured glazed pots. Or have a pool with bright coloured tiles at the bottom of it which you can see through the water.

- **Functional device**. Any active and functional object will help to enliven ch'i which is tending to slow down or stagnate. These objects include the barbecue, the lawnmower, a sundial, fountain or even the garden tap.

- **Life**. Anything which is alive will help to keep ch'i moving, even in sleepy corners of the garden. Plants are the obvious remedy here, but encouraging birds, or children, or installing a goldfish pond will have the same effect.

Features of your garden

The general layout of your garden is important. In an ideal world, your garden would have the nurturing, protective hills of the Black Tortoise to the north, the undulating downland of the Green Dragon to the east, the flat plains of the White Tiger to the west, and the sloping land of the Red Phoenix falling away gently to the south. The flat land of the Tiger in the west should be separated from your garden by a stream or small river to carry away the worst of the dangerous ch'i.

Few of us are lucky enough to have this landscape around us, but you can create it within your garden, at least on a symbolic level. If you have tall buildings to the north, these represent the high hills of the Black Tortoise. You can still dilute the ch'i from the west with a water feature in this part of the garden. In the east, why not raise the level of the garden along the boundary with a rockery or a raised bed, or some other feature such as a grassy mound or bank planted with wild flowers and bulbs? Encourage the ground level to fall away to the south by shifting a little earth around, or at least grow lower plants against the southern boundary, increasing the height of the planting as you move away from the south.

You can encourage ch'i in the way you design the layout and features of any part of the garden, in whichever enrichment they fall. Ch'i always prefers curves to straight lines, for example, except when it is sleepy or stagnant and needs to be livened up with straight-line remedies. We'll have a look at the various features you find in most gardens and identify the general guidelines for good feng shui.

Light and shade

Light and shade should be in comfortable balance in the garden. Areas of sunshine are yang and areas of shade are yin, so it is important for both to be present. There's no formula for how much shade you should have – in any case there's less shade at midday than there is in the late afternoon – you just need to think about it and concentrate on the feel of the light and shade in the garden. Does it feel too exposed, or too overshadowed?

Dappled shade is especially beneficial for ch'i, so try to create this by growing shrubs and trees with open branches which let some light through. Fruit trees such as apples are especially good for this – it's a rare orchard which doesn't have good feng shui.

Hidden corners

Although you need to have a garden which is light and open, this doesn't mean there is no room for shade, or for hidden secret corners. Quite the reverse; ch'i will want to explore parts of the garden glimpsed through a gateway or round a bend in the path as much as you do. Just make sure that the paths and corners aren't so dark or narrow that the ch'i stagnates. A garden which you cannot see all of at once is a good thing – it encourages the ch'i to flow around the whole area.

Water

Feng shui means *wind* and *water*. Wind, or air, is present in every garden, but you may need to introduce water. Ch'i loves water and water brings wildlife into a garden, which is always a good thing. The wildlife encourages ch'i which hates dead places and is drawn to life and movement.

Every garden, however small, benefits from having water in it. As we have already seen, the right kind of water feature can be used to create every one of the eight remedies. Fountains create light, sound and movement, and are functional devices; a pool of goldfish is both a stillness and a life remedy; glazed tiles or stone seen through water are an excellent colour remedy, in a pool or simply a small hanging bird bath; and water jets and channels create straight lines.

If you aren't lucky enough to have natural water in your garden, water can be introduced in realistically designed streams and waterfalls, in ponds and pools, fountains and channels, in swimming pools and in bird baths. Use natural materials to create these features; wood, stone and metal rather than plastic and concrete, as ch'i much prefers them.

You can have water in a garden even if you have small children. A fountain which bubbles up gently through stones or cobbles, or a fountainhead on the wall which spills water down on to and through cracks in paving stones, are both safe around children. Or you could have a bird bath out of children's reach – but if it stands on a pedestal make sure it is firmly attached so they can't pull the top down on to themselves.

Boundaries

You cannot control the ch'i coming from outside your garden until it reaches the boundary. It may come from an area of poor feng shui which has stagnated it or over-stimulated it. Or it may arrive as sha, or bad ch'i, imbued with a negative energy having passed through a bad area such as a graveyard, abattoir or other place of sadness or unpleasantness.

The first opportunity you get to control, improve, slow down or speed up this ch'i, is when it reaches your boundary. So you should consider the nature of the boundary in this light. Essentially, you want to encourage good ch'i, speed up slow ch'i, and calm down overactive ch'i. Look at what lies beyond each boundary and consider what kind of ch'i is reaching your garden and how you want to influence it. Think about the enrichment in which it arrives, and whether you want to change this aspect of your life.

The height and the thickness of your boundary are the main aspects which will influence ch'i as it arrives. If you want to encourage good ch'i, without affecting it strongly, use a boundary which is not too solid: a trellis with climbers, or an open-work fence such as railings, or a hedge which isn't too dense.

If you want to slow down the ch'i, use a higher or more solid boundary – or both. A brick wall, a solid fence or a dense hedge will have this effect. If you use a deciduous hedge, don't forget to consider what the effect will be in winter. To stimulate ch'i, lower the height of the boundary or open it up, with gaps cut in hedges, or a solid fence replaced with trellis.

Try to avoid a straight line along the top of your boundary. Trim your hedge with the corners rounded, or use fencing which is shaped at the top like swags. If the line is straight and hard, soften it with climbers. This applies especially in the west, where you don't want to provoke the ch'i. Don't use spiky or thorny hedges in this direction either, such as berberis or holly, but find round-leaved plants. Beech, which keeps most of its brown leaves through the winter and so remains quite dense, is a good hedging plant for north boundaries.

Gates and doors

The main entrance – and any others – should be welcoming to ch'i and visitors alike – and, of course, to you. Create an entrance which invites you to spend time in your own garden. As with boundaries, consider what influence you want to have over the ch'i as it enters your garden, and choose a gate of a suitable height and design. Solid doors block ch'i completely, and should be avoided in the west. Otherwise, when you open the gate the ch'i will rush in angrily.

You can choose wooden or metal gates, painted brightly to stimulate ch'i, or in soft colours to calm it, or left natural. A curving design in the wood or metalwork is good for ch'i, but if you want to pep up the ch'i, use a design which incorporates straight lines.

In general, gates shouldn't be left open. If the gate is needed, it should be used. The only possible exception to this is the south entrance. If a narrow or dark entrance needs opening up, an open gate is more inviting than no gate at all, and symbolises the fact that the visitor is crossing the boundary into your space. Conversely, an open south garden can acquire so much yang energy that you can't relax. When this happens, opening a gate on to land which slopes away can let out some of the excess energy and restore the garden's balance. If you do this, you may feel you need to close the gate in the winter when the southern ch'i loses some of its exuberance.

Different compass directions obviously call for different entrances, since they each bring different kinds of ch'i. Below is an idea of the type of entrance you might want in the four main compass directions.

- **South entrance.** This will let in lots of expansive yang ch'i. It's great stuff, but you can have too much of it, because it's not relaxing. Imagine looking out of the window and seeing Tigger bounding up the road to your house. You wouldn't want to shut him out, but you might want to slow him down a bit. So this gateway should be welcoming, but not wide open. Use a full-height gate with an open design, or a half-height gate with an archway over it, or a tree planted either side.

- **North entrance.** This ch'i is slow and sleepy, and needs all the encouragement it can get. This is the one direction where you might not even need a gate at all, depending on what is beyond the garden. Certainly, you should keep this entrance as open as possible and clear away any overhanging branches or plants, to encourage the ch'i. This entrance really shouldn't be in the corner of the garden. If it is, could you move it even three or four feet along the boundary towards the middle?

- **West entrance.** Don't encourage this ch'i, but don't provoke it by blocking it out completely. Use a full-height gate or door, preferably metal since that is the element of the west, which is not completely solid but not too open in design. You should also interrupt the ch'i within a few feet of the door with some object which slows it down such as a latticework screen, or a tree or shrub it has to circumnavigate.

■ **East entrance**. This is ch'i which you want to encourage with an open, welcoming entrance, preferably made of wood, which is at home in the east. However, the one risk with this kind of ch'i is that it will be so fertile that the garden becomes completely overgrown from this side. So keep a slight check on it by making sure there is a gate which is kept shut.

Paths

Generally speaking, paths should curve and flow to help the ch'i along. They should be reasonably broad, so the ch'i doesn't become stuck and stagnant. If one part of the garden is too slow and sleepy, a straight path can be used as a remedy, or a straight path with the edges softened by plants growing over them. If the ch'i is too strong, such as it often is in the west, calm it down with paths which meander and twist.

Remember that paths run in two directions. A straight path from the east will bring a rush of wise, fertile ch'i into the garden, and may be a good remedy if the west is shady and still. However, the path will also run from the west, which isn't such good news. So don't let it run up to the western boundary, or otherwise block it at that end, or start to curve it, to prevent it carrying the dangerous ch'i from the west straight back into the garden.

You can use paths to help to create a balance of texture and colour in the garden. In a shady area use a light-coloured material such as sandstone flags, or gravel, for your paths. Where the space is light and bright, you could use a darker material such as slate.

Seating

A garden should have somewhere you can sit, even if there's room only for one. You need to be able to relax. Choose seating in a suitable material and style for the direction and the flow of ch'i. Seats can be made of stone, metal, wood or even from a grass bank or a raised bed planted with thyme or camomile. Avoid synthetics such as plastic or concrete.

You can paint a seat to create a suitable colour if you need a colour remedy, and you can use a design which is predominantly straight or curved depending on whether the ch'i needs stimulating or not. A heavy, solid, stone seat or bench makes an excellent stillness remedy. You can also soften the area round a seat by turning it into an arbour. Place an arch over the top of it and grow scented climbing plants over it, such as jasmine and honeysuckle.

Beds and borders

The edges of flower beds and borders should flow in gentle lines to help the ch'i along smoothly. Avoid straight-sided beds unless you want to introduce a straight-line remedy to a particular part of the garden. Flower beds should be wide enough for the ch'i to be comfortable, but not so wide they lose their direction. Aim for between 1 and 2 metres (3 to 6 feet) depending on the proportions of the garden.

Island beds – beds which are completely surrounded by lawn or paths – should be regular in shape and preferably round, oval or octagonal, since these are the shapes ch'i likes best. Borders usually have a straight fence or wall to the rear; soften this with shrubs or climbers or it will act as a straight-line remedy even where you don't want one.

Vegetable beds tend to need straight lines in the planting, but you can still avoid too many straight lines. Use short rows of vegetables, arranged in a herringbone pattern, so they don't all funnel the ch'i the same way. You can have a circular vegetable bed divided in this way and quartered by paths, and place a large circular object in the middle, such as an earthen pot or a sundial.

Open areas

A garden needs some open, yang space to balance the yin areas. The amount depends on the size of your garden, but should be in proportion. A larger garden will need more open space than a small one. You can use a patio or lawn, or both. These areas should have curved edges, of course – round or semicircular designs are ideal – and the paths leading off them should be wide or the open ch'i won't be able to squeeze along them.

Sometimes a garden may have a large level area which is functional, such as a tennis court or swimming pool. If so, don't fence it off or – if you need to for safety reasons – make sure you have other open areas.

Paved or gravelled areas should use natural materials and not concrete – gravel, stone paving or brick are all ideal. Lawns should not be cut too low and should be broken up with flowers such as daisies and buttercups. Wild lawns, planted with wildflowers and grasses, have excellent feng shui since they attract plenty of wildlife.

Buildings

Gazebos, tool-sheds, greenhouses, pergolas and many others all have their place in the garden. Some are functional and some are decorative – and some are both. Think about where you site these buildings; make sure they are in a suitable enrichment. If you tinker about making things in your tool-shed, perhaps it should be in your friends and new beginnings area. If you have a gazebo where you and your partner like to spend long summer evenings under the stars, put it in your relationship area – or perhaps pleasure and indulgence.

Think about the proportions and shape of your garden buildings, and use as many curves as you can. Don't introduce tall, thin shapes, or sharp roof ridges, unless you want a straight-line remedy.

Don't hide functional areas in dark corners where the ch'i stagnates, or so will the garden shed and its contents. If you want to hide the building, paint it a suitable colour and grow climbers over it. Interrupt the route to it with a winding path or a fruit tree in front of it, but don't block it off completely.

Statues and ornaments

Statues and ornaments can be used to create almost any kind of remedy in the garden, and they will be there all year round, unlike many of the plants and flowers. Below is an idea of the type of objects you could use to create remedies.

- **Light**. Mirrors or glazed tiles, glass balls, garden lights or lanterns all bring light into dark areas of the garden.
- **Straight lines**. Square or rectangular planters and troughs, and any statue which uses strong, straight lines, help to revive stagnating ch'i.
- **Stillness**. Heavy, old stone troughs, millstones and saddle stones all create stillness, as do large round objects such as earthen pots and stone balls. Statues can also make good stillness remedies; use one with a relevant theme – a statue of children in the children and family enrichment, or a stone owl in the wisdom and experience area.

- ■ **Sound**. Wind chimes create sound, of course, as do strings of pebbles hung up in groups, or strings of any other natural objects you can find.
- ■ **Movement.** Wind chimes, again, or feathers threaded together, or a garden windmill, will all bring movement to the garden.
- ■ **Colour**. Glazed pots and statues, or painted wooden troughs and ornaments, all make excellent colour remedies.
- ■ **Functional device**. A sundial is an ornamental device, as is a garden windmill or a wind chime.
- ■ **Life**. You can use a bird bath or a bird table to bring life into the garden, or an ornamental urn containing a plant such as lavender which attracts bees.

Trees and plants

Trees are generally excellent for feng shui, since they are alive and attract other wildlife to them. Old trees have their own character and probably belong in your garden even more than you do, so you should never disturb them. If they are in your wisdom and experience area, think yourself lucky. Prune them, if necessary, to keep them healthy, but don't damage them.

When it comes to new trees, however, you have more control. Ch'i likes trees with a rounded shape and rounded leaves, which attract plenty of life. This makes trees such as oak, beech, apple, magnolia and horse chestnut excellent for feng shui. Tall, straight conifers are not nearly so beneficial and can be disruptive to ch'i, which can also stagnate in the dark shade around their base.

Trees such as willow, with long, thin leaves, or holly with its sharp leaves, are best in parts of the garden where the ch'i needs livening up, such as in the north. If you cut trees or hedges into topiary designs, use shapes which curve such as balls and spirals, rather than harsh squares, steps or pyramids, unless you are trying to wake up the ch'i.

Shrubs, climbers and border flowers follow the same guidelines: rounded shapes, leaves and flowers are more harmonious. Save the yucca plant for sleepy areas which need pepping up. Many plants have contrasting attributes, such as a round shape but long, thin leaves. In this case, go for the most dominant feature of the plant as this will outweigh the others. For example, lavender has spiky leaves, but this is more than countered by its rounded shape and the fact that it is evergreen, which is an excellent quality.

Scent is important in the garden. Ch'i is as attracted to a beautiful scent as we are, and this can also outweigh the handicaps of some plants. Roses, for example, have thorns which can provoke ch'i, but the shape of the flowers and the scent more than make up for this. However, this does mean that you should make sure that all the roses in your garden are scented.

Flower colour

Which colour flowers should you plant where? In places where the garden is already in balance, and the part of your life governed by that enrichment is in harmony, you should use plants with flower and foliage colours which suit the direction of the garden:

- south and south-east: bright red, orange, yellow and purple
- north: blue and creamy white
- east and north-east: green
- west and north-west: soft yellow and bright white
- south-west: rust, brown, deep red and plum, browny yellow.

In places where the ch'i needs to be stimulated, bright colours such as yellow, orange, red, strong pink and purple, and sharp white, will help to encourage it. If you want to soften and calm the ch'i, use soft blues and pinks, creamy whites and other pastels. Foliage on its own creates a cool, restful green which also slows down ch'i.

The garden through the year

Don't forget that the feng shui of your garden will influence your life for 12 months of the year, even if you use the garden for only six or eight months. So make sure that the garden is designed for good feng shui all year round.

The broad layout of your garden is important for this reason. Even when the leaves have fallen off the trees, the paths will still curve and the design of seats, gates, boundaries and ornaments will be constant. This means that such features are useful because they are permanent. A garden which relies on bedding plants all summer may look wonderful in the warm months, but it will be empty and featureless the rest of the year – and cast the same influence on your life.

The garden will open up in the winter as the leaves fall off the trees, letting in more light just as the natural light level is reduced – a perfect example of the balance of nature, and ideal feng shui. If you fill your garden with dark, evergreen trees, the effect will be too overpowering in winter. A few evergreens are good for preserving active (rather than dormant) life in the garden; but don't overdo it.

Winter plants

Keep colour in the garden for as much of the year as possible. Grow plants with rich autumn leaf colour, and shrubs such as willows and dogwoods which have brightly coloured stems in the winter. Many climbers flower in the cold months, such as witch hazel and japonica, and there are plenty of flowers which bloom in late winter, especially during mild spells, such as snowdrops, primroses and rosemary.

Make sure you have a good spread of evergreens around the garden, without dominating the area with heavy, dark trees. Herbs are ideal; plants such as rosemary and sage keep their leaves all year round. Grow lots of early-flowering plants such as hellebores and plants from spring bulbs.

Don't let the garden fall asleep

Winter is a slower, sleepier time of year than summer, for us as well as for the garden, but we aren't evolved to hibernate. We may slow the pace in winter, but we don't grind to a halt. Make sure the garden is awake all year, even if it is less active in the winter months. Make sure there is always colour and shape, and a feeling that the garden is ready to spring into life as soon as the warm weather arrives.

Keep the garden tidy through the winter. Leave seed-heads for the birds – you want to encourage them into the garden – but tidy up any dead leaves and stems, and clear away the empty flowerpots, children's toys, garden furniture and anything else which is cluttering the area or making it untidy.

It is no coincidence that most winter and early spring flowers are strongly coloured. The ch'i needs stimulating and these flowers have precisely this effect. So spread them around as much as you can, especially in the sleepier corners of the garden. You can also stimulate the ch'i with sharper, straighter shapes than you would at other times of the year. For example, a dogwood, pruned to produce straight, brightly coloured stems in winter, will stimulate ch'i. The same shrub later in the year will have oval leaves which soften the ch'i, and the stems will fade in colour and be less visible. So the same plant can produce different effects at different times of year.

The ch'i from the west is still dangerous in winter, especially if your western boundary is more open in the winter. A deciduous hedge, for example, will let through more ch'i in the winter than in the summer. So avoid putting too many sharp or spiky plants, or too many straight-stemmed shrubs, in this part of the garden.

The ch'i from the Black Tortoise in the north, on the other hand, becomes so sleepy in winter it can stagnate altogether. So this is the part of the garden to plant your straight or spiky plants, and your brightly coloured daffodils and primulas.

Don't forget to think about the eight enrichments in winter and try to keep each of them awake and active in some way. Below are a few suggestions.

- **Fame**. You will use this area every time you enter the garden. If your back garden is separate from the front and has its own fame area, make sure you visit the garden from time to time throughout the winter so that you use the fame enrichment.
- **Health and happiness**. Grow winter herbs, such as rosemary, in this part of the garden. It is also a good area for growing winter vegetables.
- **Pleasure and indulgence**. This is the place to grow something really beautiful and plentiful, with no purpose but enjoyment. Plant masses of spring bulbs here, to create a fertile riot of life in early spring. Or grow a particularly wonderful, favourite plant, which is at its best in the colder part of the year. Make it something heavily scented, such as a winter-flowering honeysuckle.

- **Friends and new beginnings**. Plant plenty of spring bulbs here to herald the new beginning of the warmer weather.

- **Relationship**. If you and your partner both enjoy being in the garden in winter, spend time in this area. If not, grow plants here which will blossom and bear fruit even in the winter months.

- **Children and family**. Children like to play outside all year round, so encourage them into this area with a cosy playhouse or activities which will keep them warm – a swing and a slide, or space to kick a football around. Whether or not you have children, you can extend your circle to include a whole family of birds if you put out nuts, seeds, bread and scraps for them in the cold weather. This is a good enrichment in which to put a bird table.

- **Wisdom and experience**. A compost heap in this area will mature throughout the winter, even if you can't see it happening. You can visit it from time to time with kitchen waste to add to it.

- **Wealth**. Store any garden furniture or equipment here, so the enrichment has a use throughout the winter.

Tiny gardens

Even if your garden is only a few feet across – perhaps a balcony – or even smaller, you can still improve its feng shui. You can create an excellent feng shui garden in a window box with just a little thought and effort. Below are the most important ways of improving even the smallest of gardens.

- Keep it tidy. Clear up the clutter and mend any broken boundary fences or gates.

- Create curves and soft edges. Many small gardens are square or rectangular yards with high walls or fences. This doesn't offer any of the curving shapes which ch'i likes, so you will have to add them. You might be able to replace the gate with one which has a curved or rounded design on it, or put an archway over it. Hard surfaces such as paving or concrete can be replaced (or covered over) with something softer such as brick, perhaps laid in circles radiating out from the centre, or with gravel.

- Add a few plants, even if only a couple of climbers in pots to soften the corners of the yard, or a hanging basket or two with trailing plants. Or grow plants in the cracks between paving stones. Throw a few packets-worth of seeds around, of plants like cornflowers, wallflowers or love-in-a-mist, which will happily grow in this kind of environment.

- Introduce colour to the garden, either with plants or with glazed, coloured flower pots or ornaments. Or you could paint a wall, trellis or gate in a bright colour.

- Create a water feature, even if it is just a small goldfish pond a couple of feet across, or a bird bath.

- Bring sound into the garden with a fountain or water spout, or something as simple as a wind chime outside the back door.

- If you haven't much room – or time – for plants, how about creating interest with a collection of driftwood and beautiful stones you've found? Or a group of outdoor lanterns? Just make sure you keep these things clean and tidy, and don't allow them to become hidden by dead leaves in the autumn.

- Now you've created a space that is enjoyable to spend time in, put a seat there. Find a suitable bench or chair, made of natural material such as wood or metal, and in a shape and design which will help the ch'i to flow through and around it.

Even the smallest garden can be a place where you can enjoy spending time, and which will influence your life for the better. A tidy, pleasant space, designed to help the ch'i flow smoothly, shouldn't be beyond anyone's capability. It will reward you a hundredfold for the effort that goes into creating it, giving you a new area to enjoy yourself which brings happiness and good fortune to every part of your life.

7 | FENG SHUI FOR WORK AND BUSINESS

Whether you work for someone else or for yourself, feng shui has a huge effect on your life. We spend a vast proportion of our time at work and, for many of us, it is a vital aspect of our lives. So it's worth doing what we can to improve our income, our job satisfaction and our working relationships. Feng shui can improve your life if you work for someone else or if you run your own business, small or large, and this chapter is all about how to make the most of it.

Feng shui at work

If you work for an employer, you probably have no control over which direction your office faces, whether you share it with someone else, how many floors up in the building it is, and so on. You do, however, have control over your own office space and your desk. It is the area which you can influence and which, in turn, can influence your life.

So the first thing to do, as ever, is to lay the Pah Kwa over a plan of your area of influence, whether it's the whole office or simply the desk. Find out where each of the enrichments lies. The eight enrichments will apply to work areas of your life, so they won't have the same influence as the enrichments in your home or garden. Below is a run-down of the areas of your working life that each enrichment will govern.

- **Fame**. This is about your reputation at work, within the office and beyond. Good feng shui in the fame enrichment will help to win you notice and respect from your colleagues, superiors and customers.
- **Health and happiness**. If this area has problems or is cluttered you are likely to find work stressful or unfulfilling.
- **Pleasure and indulgence**. As you would expect, this enrichment governs those areas of work which you most

enjoy. This might well be those long, boozy lunches, or the socialising after hours, or the weeks when the boss is away. It could also be any real work which you find particularly enjoyable. This area is usually most dominant in the offices of people who thoroughly enjoy their work.

■ **Friends and new beginnings**. This area influences your social relationships at work, and also new projects or responsibilities.

■ **Relationship**. Your key relationship at work is governed by this enrichment. Only you know which relationship is the most important to you, but it is usually your relationship with either your boss or your assistant.

■ **Children and family**. These are symbolic children and you will probably know what they are, although they differ between all of us. If you are a salesperson, they are often your customers, whom you are there to look after and nurture. For a researcher, they will be all the reports which have been put together so lovingly. For an accountant, they may be all the neat ledgers – or computer printouts – which are the result of all the work.

■ **Wisdom and experience**. This enrichment governs your knowledge, learning and training, and therefore has a big influence over your career and promotion, which are determined by your experience.

■ **Wealth**. This area, unsurprisingly, is all to do with your salary – along with any bonuses, or extras such as a company car or extra holiday entitlement.

Your office

You should pay as much attention to the layout of your office as you do to the layout of your kitchen, bedroom, sitting room or garden. The first and most important thing is to make sure that you don't sit with your back to a door. You can't relax and concentrate on work if you can't see who is coming and going behind you. So start by positioning the desk somewhere you can see the door (or doors) from (see Figure 7.1).

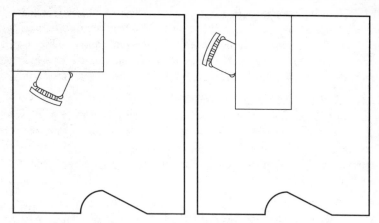

Figure 7.1 Examples of a poor desk position (left) and a good desk position (right)

You calculate the enrichments for your office in the same way as for your rooms at home. Lay the Pah Kwa over the plan of the office with the fame enrichment facing whichever way the room faces. This is normally towards the windows – the eyes of the building – but you may intuitively feel that this isn't the case in your office. Of course, some offices have no windows – especially an open-plan office area created using room-divider screens – but even those with small windows may face a more dominant door.

Place the desk in an enrichment which is appropriate to the work you do, but not in your pleasure and indulgence area or you won't do any work at all. You might choose to put it in your wealth enrichment if you're a salesperson, your friends and new beginnings area if you're a manager, your relationship area if you're a PA, your wisdom and experience enrichment if you're a data processor, and so on. If you can't place it in your first choice of enrichment for some reason – perhaps it would block the door – find another area which is also suitable.

As with your rooms at home, make your office as light and bright as you can. Bring any dark corners into the room using lights or mirrors, and soften any sharp corners which jut into the room using plants or some other object – you could put a hook here and hang your coat on it, for example.

A large proportion of offices are square, or almost square, which is good for feng shui. However, some do have enrichments missing. If you are missing an important enrichment such as wealth, or health and happiness, hang a mirror on the wall in the place where the enrichment should be to create depth and the illusion that the room continues behind the wall.

Once you have established where the enrichments fall, and positioned your desk in the best place possible, you can position the rest of your furniture and equipment. Make sure you choose an appropriate enrichment for each item. Below are some ideas for positioning the most common office equipment and furniture which isn't sitting on your desk (we'll look at that later).

- **Fax machine**. This can go in your friends and new beginnings area, since it is a prime source of contact with other people.
- **Filing cabinet**. This might go in wisdom and experience if you file data and archive material, but customer files might do better in children and family, or in wealth if they are the mainstay of your sales operation.
- **Bookshelf**. Most reference books belong in wisdom and experience, but some books and directories might be more suited to friends and new beginnings.
- **Easy chairs**. These should go in your health and happiness area, or possibly in pleasure and indulgence.
- **Wall planner**. If this records when you are going to be out and about in the world, at exhibitions and presentations, it would be well suited to the fame area. On the other hand, it might tell you when all your projects are scheduled for, in which case friends and new beginnings would be more appropriate.
- **Computer console**. If your computer isn't on your desk, site it somewhere suitable. If you use it for retrieving data, for example, position it in your wisdom and experience area.

Sharing an office

If you share an office with a colleague, boss or assistant, you both need to position your desks in a suitable place, without your backs to the door. One arrangement which often works extremely well is to arrange your desks so that each is across a corner of the wall facing the door. If you place your desk across a corner, however, make sure the corner behind you is used for something and doesn't become a dead area where the ch'i stagnates. Another good desk arrangement in a shared office is to place the desks so that they form a T or L-shape.

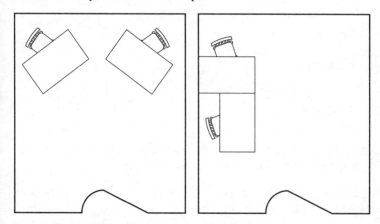

Figure 7.2   Two good desk layouts for a shared office

The further you are from the door, and the more directly you face it, the more dominant your position is. So if there are two desks in an office which are not exactly symmetrical in position, the one furthest away from the door, and most opposite to it, will be in the more superior position. If you are the boss and you share an office with your assistant, make sure you have the more superior placement for your desk if you want your authority acknowledged.

In a small office there may not be room for you both to occupy the same enrichment, so you will need to decide where you should each be. If one of you works for the other, as an assistant or secretary, their desk can be in the relationship area since their main focus is on the other person. Or you may be concerned with different aspects of the job anyway – one of you might be concerned with selling (and would do well in the wealth area) while the other deals more with the customer care back-up (which is suited to the children and family area).

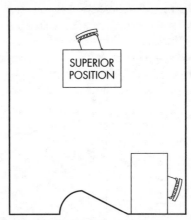

Figure 7.3   This office has two desks, one of which is in a more superior position than the other

Even if you both do the same work, you should find at least two enrichments which are appropriate, and you often find that your different personalities dictate which one is most appropriate for each of you. If you both work in marketing, for example, one of you might be better at promotion and image-making, while the other has stronger organisational skills. The image-maker would thrive in the fame enrichment, while the organiser would be better placed in the friends and new beginnings area.

Your desk

Your desk should always be neat and tidy, with a minimum of clutter. File papers and documents, put your hole puncher and stapler in a drawer, and free up some space on the desktop. If you want your working life to be clear and focused, set yourself an example with your desk.

There are certain items and objects you will still need to keep on your desk, and you should make sure that these are in a suitable enrichment. Lay the Pah Kwa over a plan of your desk, with fame in the position where you sit, and see where on your desk the other enrichments fall. Now find a suitable place for the items which are staying on your desk. Below are a few examples.

■ **Computer**. If you use this chiefly to store data, you could position it in the wisdom and experience section of the desk.

If you use it to make your money – as a designer or advertising copywriter, for example – it could go in the wealth enrichment.

■ **Computer disks**. The material on disks represents children to some people – all your completed projects. If this is the case, put them in the children and family enrichment. If they are concerned with new projects, put them in the friends and new beginnings enrichment. If they store information for reference, keep them in the wisdom and experience area.

■ **Telephone**. This is often suited to friends and new beginnings, but if you sell over the phone, the wealth enrichment would be a better place for it.

■ **Paper – notepad, telephone message pad, Post-it notes**. These generally belong in friends and new beginnings, although if you use your notepad for certain types of notes, there may be a better place for it. For example, if you find longhand writing therapeutic, as many people do, you might prefer to keep your notepad in your health and happiness area.

■ **Reference files and books**. These usually belong in wisdom and experience.

■ **Tea or coffee mug**. This is a good thing to keep in the pleasure and indulgence area.

■ **Diary**. This belongs in friends and new beginnings ideally, although if it chiefly lists appointments with customers you might prefer to keep it in your children and family area, or in your wealth area.

■ **Address book**. If this is separate from your diary, keep it in your friends and new beginnings area. If both are in the same book or file, you probably have your entire identity bound up in it, so you'd better keep it in your fame enrichment.

■ **Personal photographs of partner or children**. Many people find this an inspiring thing to have on the desk – and so it should be. Often these people are the reason you are working. Keep their photos in the children and family section of your desk, or the relationship section.

Using feng shui to resolve problems

Many of the persistent problems you encounter in an office environment will be resolved through applying feng shui principles to your office space and your desk. But some of them depend on co-operation from other people and, in this case, you need to look at how you can use feng shui to influence them.

Concentrate on the relevant enrichment of your office and of your desk. When the problems concern your closest work colleague – usually your boss or your assistant – focus on the relationship area. Otherwise, look at the friends and new beginnings enrichment. First, make sure this area is in order, has no clutter or dark corners, and nothing inappropriate in it. For example, a waste bin in your relationship area could indicate that you are throwing away the opportunities for a good working relationship. (Move it to friends and new beginnings where it will symbolise clearing out the old to make way for the new.)

Now you want to introduce something to this enrichment which represents the change you want to bring about in the other person. You'll have to use your imagination and intuition, because we can't list every possible problem here, but below are a few examples.

- Your assistant persistently delivers work late: put a clock in the relationship enrichment.
- One of your colleagues never prepares data accurately for you to work from: place a relevant reference book in the friends and new beginnings area.
- Your boss is spiky and difficult to get along with: put a soft, cuddly toy bear in the relationship area.
- Your secretary is always lacking in enthusiasm and energy for new ideas: put a party popper, or a picture of a firework, in your relationship enrichment.
- Your colleagues are always pooh-poohing your ideas and undervaluing your contribution: put a small set of balancing scales in your friends and new beginnings enrichment to persuade them to weigh up your suggestions before they reject them.

Feng shui in business

When you run your own business, either alone or with other people, you have control over far more than your own office. You decide where you should run the business from, and what the general plan of the whole building should be.

Siting your business

If you haven't yet set up your business, or if you need to move into new premises, you should make sure you choose a site which has good feng shui. The first thing to do is to consider the history of the building, since it has its own ch'i just as we have our own internal ch'i. The building's ch'i will be influenced by what has happened in it before, so you need to make sure it has a positive track record. If the previous businesses located in it have failed, this is a bad sign. However, if the building is being vacated because the business it houses has grown too big and successful for it, this suggests that the place will have positive ch'i of its own.

Look at the entrance to the building – the one your customers will see – dispassionately. Is it welcoming? Does it invite you to enter? If a lick of paint is the most it needs, the building looks promising, but if it is run down, and the surrounding buildings are drab and dirty, your customers and your employees are likely to be put off. This may sound to you like common sense rather than feng shui, but in fact a large part of feng shui *is* common sense. Going through the discipline of feng shui often helps us to see what we should have seen anyway, but didn't.

Feng shui and roads

Ch'i flows down roads, so the position of your building in relation to the nearby roads is important. According to feng shui, roads are the modern equivalent of rivers. Few of us now live near rivers, especially in cities, but roads carry ch'i in exactly the same way, so a gently meandering road is the best.

A road pointing straight at your offices, shop or factory will funnel the ch'i too fast and it could become dangerous and unpredictable. Two or more roads pointing at you are even worse. Dead ends have the opposite effect – the ch'i is inclined to stagnate and your business is unlikely to grow.

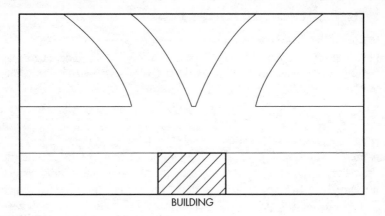

BUILDING

Figure 7.4   Roads pointing at your building are bad feng shui

The ideal location is on a corner with a road running past the door, preferably a road with gentle curves in it, rather than a dead straight road which allows the ch'i to rush past without stopping.

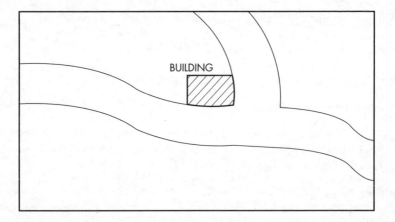

BUILDING

Figure 7.5   An ideal location for a business is on a corner of a gently winding road

Where should you locate each department?

Once you have chosen the building – or if you are already there – work out the enrichments in the usual way, by laying the Pah Kwa over a plan of the building, placing the front entrance (the one visitors and customers use, if you have more than one entrance) in the fame enrichment. The front entrance and any reception area just inside it are your public face, so they belong in the fame enrichment.

Now locate the other functions of your business in the most appropriate enrichments. Put your money, or your accounts department, or your till if you run a shop, in the wealth enrichment (if you put it in pleasure and indulgence you're likely to spend all your profits). Put the records department in wisdom and experience, sales could go in children and family, and marketing in friends and new beginnings. Or marketing could go in the fame enrichment on the first floor, above reception.

It's not a good idea to occupy only upstairs floors in a tall building; it's hard for the ch'i to reach your offices. You should aim to use the ground floor and only use upper floors if you also control the ch'i in the floors below. That way you can make sure the stairways are wide, clean, fresh and welcoming, with plenty of light, and mirrors on any bends if necessary, to encourage the ch'i upstairs.

The further from the ground each department is, the less public a face it should have. It's much better to put sales and marketing lower down, and research or strategic planning functions higher up the building. It is no coincidence that in organisations where the most senior directors have their offices on the top floor, the management are often accused of being out of touch. It's because they are. It's far better to put the board room and the MD's office on the ground floor.

Layout and design

All the basic rules of feng shui which we looked at in Chapter 5 apply in offices as much as houses: doors should be hung so they don't open on to walls, long corridors should be broken up, sharp corners should be softened and dark areas should be brightened up. Large blank areas of wall should be decorated with pictures, awards, wall planners or something which breaks up the starkness.

Your staff will respond to the surroundings in which they work – it's human nature. If you put them in small, cramped offices with little light which are in need of redecorating, they will be less productive. So make sure that all your employees work in an environment which you'd be happy to work in yourself – even if you rarely visit the basement or wherever it is you've put them. To work well, all your employees need the following amenities.

- **Light**. Preferably natural, but if it's artificial light, at least make sure there's plenty of it.
- **Space**. Find a way to make sure that there is room for everyone to move comfortably, or the ch'i won't be able to either.
- **Personal space**. As well as a general feeling of space, people also need their own territory where they feel they are in control. I know of one office where, rather than move into new premises, the management tried to keep costs down by putting two people into offices which had been intended for only one. When this seemed to work, they crammed a third person in to many of the rooms as the company expanded. In the end they had one room in which five people were squeezed into a one-person office, and they felt pleased with themselves. The five people, however, weren't so pleased. They could hardly get any work done and within six months, four of them had left the company. What's more, the company's fortunes began to go downhill quickly.
- **Freshness**. People need a clean, fresh work space which they feel happy in. Update rickety, depressing old furniture and give the place a lick of paint. Use a touch of colour in a shade which suits the direction in which the building faces, or in a shade which will influence the workforce. In a laid-back environment, a touch of bright red or orange will stimulate people; in a frenetic, high-pressure atmosphere you can help to calm people with gentle blues and greens.

We looked at individual offices earlier in this chapter, but it's worth mentioning open-plan layouts. These are excellent, if designed well. The ch'i likes to be able to flow comfortably, and knocking several small offices into one big space is a good way to achieve this. However, ch'i doesn't like huge empty spaces, so open-plan offices should incorporate some divisions, perhaps using office divider screens, which are just above eye level but don't reach the ceiling.

This means each employee, or each group of two or three, has their own space. You need to treat this space as you would an office; don't place desks so that workers have their backs to the open side of their section, and make sure they all have plenty of space. It's better to sit people in small groups in a comfortably sized area than to give everybody their own tiny, cramped space. If you feel that the whole area is pleasant to walk around, and that each area is interesting to visit, and you are encouraged to look round the next corner into the next space, the ch'i will also feel welcome and happy to flow in and out and around the building.

Using feng shui to resolve staff problems

We saw earlier how you can influence the people around you to be more co-operative by using feng shui. Well, if you're the boss, you have a far greater range of options at your disposal. For a start, you should adopt a system which stipulates that every office should be kept neat and tidy. If one or two offices are a mess, with piles of papers all over the floor, the ch'i will bypass them and flow on to a more welcoming area.

Make a rule that everyone should tidy their desk – properly – before they go home each evening. Don't wield a stick, use a carrot: give an award each month for the tidiest desk. Send people on courses, if necessary, to teach them how to control paperwork and operate an efficient, tidy system. Hold a 'clear your desk' day twice a year: everyone should be in the office, with no meetings planned, for a morning or afternoon and should produce as many sacks of rubbish as possible. They should sort through all the papers at the bottom of the in-tray, all the records in their filing cabinets which they no longer need, and so on.

You can also move people around to make sure that they work in the best position.

- If an employee is a bad time-keeper, sit them under the clock. If they tend to get away from work early, put them somewhere from where they can't see the door.
- An employee who takes a lot of time off sick can be moved to a desk in the health and happiness enrichment.

- The friends and new beginnings area is a good place to put someone who is difficult to get on with; and make sure the ch'i can move freely in and out of their office without stagnating or being accelerated.
- If one of your employees is picky and over-careful with work, perhaps being so thorough that they don't get through as much work as they should, put them in the pleasure and indulgence enrichment to loosen them up a bit.

If work plays a big part in your life, and the money, status or pleasure it brings is important to you, good feng shui at work is every bit as crucial as good feng shui at home. Even if you control no more space than your own desk, you can use feng shui to improve your working life. And if you run your own business, feng shui can give its success a massive boost.

8 FENG SHUI AND YOUR LIFE

So far we've examined how you can look at a house, garden, workplace or anywhere else and improve its feng shui to create the most beneficial influence on you. However, you may want to start from the other end, by first identifying the problems in your life which need addressing, and then finding changes you can make to your surroundings to create the effect you want.

You can use feng shui effectively in this way, and that's what this chapter is all about. Using feng shui to do a room-by-room audit of your home and workplace will have a significant impact for the better on your life. Some things, however, are better resolved by starting with the problem because they deal with more than one room or enrichment, or because they involve, for example, different personalities of people living in the same house.

Feng shui and relationships

Relationship problems are one of the greatest stress factors in our lives, and curing them can bring a level of peace and happiness which simply can't be provided by money, good health or anything else. Whether the problem is in your relationship with your partner, your mother, your children or your friends, you can use feng shui to change things for the better.

You and your partner

You need to concentrate on your relationship enrichment. Where in the house is it? Its natural home is in the north of the house, where it receives the nurturing ch'i of the Black Tortoise, but unless your house faces south, it will fall in a different part of the house. So what kind of ch'i will your relationship be receiving? This is obviously going to affect the nature of your relationship. Each of the eight compass directions brings its own ch'i, and each of these types of ch'i can manifest in either a positive or a negative way, depending on the feng shui of the area it has travelled through to get there, and the room or area itself.

If the enrichment faces the White Tiger in the west, for example, the ch'i may be either changeable or dangerous. If it is dangerous, the relationship is likely to be stormy. If this is you, and you want to calm things down a bit, make sure your relationship enrichment has plenty of stillness remedies – the type which are best suited to the west of the house. If you control the area outside the house in this direction – if the ch'i travels through your garden – add stillness remedies here as well.

Let's run through the eight house directions and you can check which kind of ch'i your relationship enrichment is receiving, and what remedy is best suited to it.

House faces...	Relationship enrichment	Type of ch'i (positive/negative)	Suitable remedy
South	North	Nurturing/lingering	Movement
South-west	North-east	Flourishing/ stagnating	Colour
West	East	Growing/ overpowering	Functional device
North-west	South-east	Creative/provoking	Life
North	South	Vigorous/ accelerating	Light
North-east	South-west	Soothing/ disruptive	Straight lines
East	West	Changeable/ dangerous	Stillness
South-east	North-west	Expansive/ unpredictable	Sound

This table should help you to identify the problem areas in your relationship, and find ways to resolve them. Introduce the remedies which will bring out the positive aspect of the ch'i which influences your relationship.

Bedrooms in the relationship enrichment

You also need to consider which room, or rooms (inevitably, if you have an upstairs), fall in your relationship enrichment. This should tell you a good deal about it. If the spare bedroom falls in the enrichment, for example, rather than your own bedroom, this suggests that your relationship is an aside to the rest of your life. Could you swap bedrooms? Or at least could you and your partner sleep in the spare room from time to time?

If your relationship enrichment occupies one of your children's bedrooms, your children are likely to play a big part in the relationship. If they are a positive factor, that's fine. But if they are the cause of arguments – perhaps because they are children of only one of you, from a previous relationship – you will need to take action. If you can move them out of your relationship area, this will ease a lot of pressure on you. If you can't, represent the relationship area in your own bedroom by adding movement, the remedy which is most at home in the relationship enrichment. Add a clock, a wind chime in the window, or even a lava lamp. This will give your relationship an identity which doesn't include your children, as well as the one which does.

The bathroom

If your relationship enrichment occupies the bathroom, it makes a lot of difference how you use the bathroom. If you rush into it, do what you have to as fast as possible and then rush out again, your relationship is likely to be treated in the same way. Use the bathroom for relaxing and enjoying yourself. Take trouble over it – redecorate and find a few carefully chosen ornaments for it. Use matching towels which look smart and cared for, and hang them up neatly when you're not using them. And keep the lavatory seat down – don't flush away your relationship.

The sitting room

The sitting room is a relaxed, comfortable room, which bodes well for your relationship. But if things aren't right in the room, your relationship won't be as happy and relaxed as it should be. Do you spend much time in your sitting room, or are you always busy elsewhere? Make sure you give this enrichment as much of your time as it deserves.

Where is the focus of your sitting room? It should be on the other people in it, when they are there. If it is actually on the television so that you rarely if ever give other people your full attention, your relationship is bound to suffer. It will be treated as a distraction or an afterthought, rather than as one of the essential ingredients in your happiness. Turn off the television, except for the occasional programme you have specially planned to watch, and concentrate on the people with whom you are sharing the room.

Sitting rooms should not be too cluttered with furniture, or there is no room for manoeuvre. If you can hardly move around your sitting room, you're likely to find that your relationship suffers in the same way – when there are problems you find it hard to work round them; they tend to sit unmovingly in your way.

The dining room

Many people rarely use their dining rooms – only when they have company. However, when they do use them, they make a special effort. This position for your relationship enrichment can work well if you don't live with your partner, and perhaps see them only occasionally but make an effort for them when you do. If your relationship is an everyday one, however, the enrichment needs an everyday room. So make sure you go into the dining room regularly. Start eating at least one meal a day in there, or keep plants in there which need regular watering. Or put the telephone in there – especially if you often speak to your partner by phone.

Another danger with dining rooms is that, because they may not be used often for eating in, they acquire another use. The dining room becomes a part-time study, or the children's homework room, or gets used for storage. I even know of one family which uses their dining room to house a collection of 15 gerbils in cages, along with sacks of straw and bags of food.

This may not matter if the other use for the room is appropriate to the enrichment, and if the room is kept clean and tidy, the way ch'i likes it. A children's homework room here, for example, is fine. The children are a central part of your relationship anyway, and the homework is probably cleared away without trace once it's done, leaving the room neat and tidy.

However, many secondary uses for a dining room create untidiness (even without gerbils). Suppose your dining room doubles as a study. A dining room tends to contain little functional furniture apart from a table and chairs. This means your papers, books, phone directories, pens and other bits and pieces have nowhere to live except out on the table, in a mess. It would be far better to abandon the dining room completely if you barely use it, and convert the room into a proper study, with a desk, drawers, shelves and bookcases. Or create room for proper study furniture by replacing the existing dining table with a smaller one, or one with drop-sides so you can store it more efficiently. Perhaps you could clear more space by keeping some of the dining chairs elsewhere, and bringing them in to the dining room only when you are entertaining.

The kitchen

There's a saying that the kitchen is the heart of the home. If this is true in your case, this is a lovely room to have in your relationship enrichment, but for many people, the kitchen is rarely used, perhaps simply because it is too small. These are the people who risk problems with their relationships.

Make your kitchen as pleasant as you possibly can. The chief aim is to spend longer in the kitchen, and to encourage your partner to spend time in there with you. It's no good if the time is spent reluctantly washing up or peeling the potatoes; make the kitchen the place where you choose to sit and drink a cup of coffee.

If you have room for a table in your kitchen which you can eat at, make sure there is one, at least for breakfast and lunch (you may use the dining room for your really relaxed meal at the end of the day), and make the effort to eat together – this is essential. If the kitchen's main function is food and eating, you must share these with your partner as much as possible.

If you haven't room for a proper table, can you at least find the space for a small table, or a couple of comfortable chairs for taking a coffee break together? Even one comfortable chair would mean that while one of you is cooking, the other can sit and chat. If your relationship is drifting and you feel separate from your partner it's often worth forgoing a few cupboards to create the space for this, or moving the washing machine or freezer into the garage or another room.

Now you have somewhere to sit, create an atmosphere which makes you want to sit there. Replace your old kitchen units, or at least give them an overhaul. Fix all the broken hinges. Redecorate, using a welcoming colour which is not too bright – you need to relax in the kitchen. Try pale green or blue, or perhaps a soft primrose yellow, depending on the direction of the room. Add pretty curtains if you've never got round to it before, and treat yourself to a new set of mugs or plates which aren't covered in cracks and chips.

Connecting areas

Sometimes relationships have a problem which is caused by the fact that the relationship is too separate from the rest of your life, or some parts of it. Perhaps the relationship suffers because you never have time to spend just enjoying each other's company. Or your partner doesn't understand your work and isn't interested, and you want them to be more involved. Or perhaps your partner doesn't want to meet any of your friends or your family.

If your relationship enrichment occupies a part of the house which is cut off from the rest of the building, this often accounts for the problem. It may be at the far end of a long corridor, or in an annexe, or in the garage. Or it may simply be cut off from the relevant enrichment – if you have no time to enjoy yourselves together, perhaps the pleasure and indulgence enrichment is cut off.

Whether it is the relationship enrichment which is cut off or the one representing the part of your life which is too separate from your relationship, the solution is to bring these two together. If you can, leave doors open to allow a better flow of ch'i between these parts of the house, or move any large, cumbersome piece of furniture which may be blocking it. If the relationship enrichment is in the garage, add a connecting door to the house. If you can, keep this door unlocked as much as possible, and lock the front door of the garage instead.

If you can't free up the flow of ch'i as much as you need to, you can find other ways of linking the two areas. You could find two matching objects, or a pair – candlesticks, matching clocks, a pair of porcelain statues, nesting tables – and place one in each enrichment to create a link. Or you could decorate the two areas in the same colour, or variations on the same colour; one room might be blue and white and the other blue and yellow, but both using the same blue.

What if you're single?

Of course, you may be free and single. If so, and that's how you like it, don't change anything in your relationship enrichment (if you even have one). However, many single people would prefer to find a partner who complements and supports them. If this applies to you, what can you do?

People in this situation often have no relationship enrichment in their house. If this is the case, remedy it in the ways we saw in Chapter 5. Use mirrors to create the appearance of a relationship enrichment, and remember to do this on every floor of the house, not only the ground floor.

Your relationship enrichment (whether actual or reflected) should be entirely free of clutter and mess. If you can't remove or throw away the clutter, find a way to tidy it. Move a cupboard or shelves into the room to hold it all neatly. As we saw earlier, see what kind of ch'i your relationship area receives, and make sure you have plenty of remedies for any potential bad ch'i, or sha.

You also need to place something – or more than one thing – in your relationship enrichment which represents the relationship you would like. Living, growing plants symbolise a growing partnership, and it is all the better if you choose one which blossoms and even bears fruit. Don't choose a sharp or spiky plant – a cactus is a bad idea. Remember to pay attention to the relationship area of your garden as well, if you have one. Outdoor plants in the relationship area should include evergreens, and use perennial plants rather than annuals, which die at the end of each year.

You can also place an object in the enrichment which represents the qualities you most want to find in a relationship. If you want someone who will be bright and cheerful and help you to lighten up your life, you could use a shiny object, or a side light, or a cushion in a shimmering fabric, or keep your sparkling earrings and necklaces on display. If you want someone who will love you and form a close partnership with you, hang a picture of two swans entwined (since swans mate for life), or place a 3-D interlocking puzzle, which once joined together are almost impossible to separate again. So think about the quality which matters most to you, and represent this in your relationship enrichment.

You and your friends

When it comes to improving your relationships with your friends and family, the same principles apply. First, you need to establish where the relevant enrichment lies, and what sort of ch'i it receives from its compass direction. Then you can apply a suitable remedy to the area to help the ch'i flow more harmoniously.

Suppose you find that a lot of your friendships are too unpredictable for you – very off and on – and some of your friends are inclined to go into sulks with you one week, and be all over you the next. You may well find that your friends and new beginnings enrichment is in the north-west of your house. It is at home here, but the expansive ch'i can degenerate into unpredictable sha if the feng shui is wrong. So you would need to use a sound remedy, since this is the best kind of remedy in the north-west. You could add a ticking clock or a wind chime, or put a radio in this part of the house.

Below is a table to work out which direction your friends and family enrichment is in, what kind of ch'i it receives, and what remedy would be most suitable if you feel that your friendships are suffering from the negative form of ch'i which comes from this direction.

House faces...	Friends and new beginnings enrichment	Type of ch'i (positive/ negative)	Suitable remedy
South	North-west	Expansive/ unpredictable	Sound
South-west	North	Nurturing/lingering	Movement
West	North-east	Flourishing/stagnating	Colour
North-west	East	Growing/ overpowering	Functional device
North	South-east	Creative/provoking	Life
North-east	South	Vigorous/ accelerating	Light
East	South-west	Soothing/ disruptive	Straight lines
South-east	West	Changeable/ dangerous	Stillness

As with your relationship with your partner, you should check the feng shui of the relevant area and do what you can to improve it. Think about the room in question, and go through the same process we outlined earlier. If your friends and new beginnings enrichment includes a room which is cluttered, do you have more friends than you can keep up with? If so, tidy the room and clear out some of the furniture.

Make sure that if your friends are important to you, you spend time in your friends and new beginnings enrichment. Give yourself a reason to visit it – perhaps this is the place to put your telephone.

If your friends are a cause of stress, analyse why and place an object in this enrichment which will represent the relationship you would like to have with them. For example, if your friends are always pressuring you to take advice when you don't want to, and are always telling you what to do, you might decide that you would like to be able to resist them more easily, and be strong enough to ignore their pressure without it distressing you. You might also like to find new friends who are more understanding of the way you are, and less judgemental. Therefore, you want to find objects which represent strength and understanding. You could symbolise strength with a statue of an ox, or something made of iron, and understanding could be represented by a picture of an eye, to indicate insight, or by a set of balancing scales.

Link your friends and new beginnings enrichment to another enrichment if you feel the two are out of touch. If your friends and your partner never see eye to eye, decorate these two parts of your house in complementary styles, and find paired objects, such as matching side lights, which you can split and put one in each enrichment.

You and your family

When it comes to your family, rather than your friends, you need to go through exactly the same process but with the children and family enrichment rather than friends and new beginnings. If your mother is always too domineering, perhaps your children and family area is in the east where bad ch'i forms overpowering sha. Remedying the feng shui will return it to growing ch'i, and your mother will start to support rather than dominate you.

Below is the table for locating your children and family enrichment, establishing what kind of ch'i or sha it receives, and identifying the best type of remedy for bringing the feng shui of this area into balance.

House faces...	Children and family enrichment	Type of ch'i (positive/ negative)	Suitable remedy
South	North-east	Flourishing/ stagnating	Colour
South-west	East	Growing/ overpowering	Functional device
West	South-east	Creative/ provoking	Life
North-west	South	Vigorous/ accelerating	Light
North	South-west	Soothing/ disruptive	Straight lines
North-east	West	Changeable/ dangerous	Stillness
East	North-west	Expansive/ unpredictable	Sound
South-east	North	Nurturing/ lingering	Movement

Once again, make sure you use this part of your house more if your family is not as close as you would like, and keep it clear and tidy. If you have a specific problem in your relationship with any of your family, put a relevant object in the enrichment. You might want to encourage your mother to leave you alone by placing a picture or representation of a loving mother smiling at her child.

Feng shui and money

Your money is governed by the wealth enrichment, so this is the one to concentrate on if all is not as it should be. Feng shui cannot make everyone a millionaire, but it can give you the best chance of maximising your money. It can bring luck, it can improve your earning potential, and it can create a better atmosphere for you to spend or save your money wisely.

So the first stage, as always, is to locate your wealth enrichment. Once you know where it is, you know from the compass direction what kind of ch'i is reaching that part of your house or garden. Is it positive ch'i or negative sha? If you feel it is negative sha, the following table also tells you which type of remedy is best suited to that direction.

House faces...	Wealth enrichment	Type of ch'i (positive/ negative)	Suitable remedy
South	South-east	Creative/provoking	Life
South-west	South	Vigorous/accelerating	Light
West	South-west	Soothing/disruptive	Straight lines
North-west	West	Changeable/ dangerous	Stillness
North	North-west	Expansive/ unpredictable	Sound
North-east	North	Nurturing/lingering	Movement
East	North-east	Flourishing/stagnating	Colour
South-east	East	Growing/ overpowering	Functional device

Suppose your wealth enrichment is in the north-west of your house. This would bring expansive ch'i, which is just what you want in your wealth area. But if the ch'i degenerates to sha, it becomes unpredictable. So your finances will follow, and you may find that your income fluctuates enormously and unexpectedly – or if your income is steady, your outgoings are unexpectedly up and down, placing you in worrying financial straits at times. So improve the feng shui of this area to replenish the supply of beneficial, expansive ch'i.

Wherever your money enrichment falls, make sure that the rooms it occupies are clear and uncluttered, and include representations of wealth. Place a few coins in a box in the room, or put a tank or bowl of goldfish (which represent money) in the area – this is especially beneficial if your wealth enrichment falls in the south-east, where life remedies are the best ones to use.

If you find you are inclined to spend money too fast, you will need to calm down the ch'i in your wealth area. Make sure it isn't too open, and although you shouldn't clutter it with furniture, place one or two items strategically so that you cannot move round the room without having to slow down once or twice to manoeuvre. If the room has two doors, especially if you tend to go in through one and straight out through the other, it's not surprising if your money comes in and goes straight out again. Keep the doors shut, and obstruct the route from one to the other with a table in the middle of the room, or a chair against a wall between the two doors.

If your finances are very complicated, make a special effort to tidy and organise your wealth area in order to keep as much clarity as possible. Suppose your bedroom falls in this area. Don't simply tidy your clothes away into drawers and wardrobes – organise them as well. Put trousers at one end of the wardrobe and shirts at the other; put T-shirts at the other end of the drawer from cardigans; separate socks and tights in your underwear drawer, and so on.

Feng shui and health

If you suffer from persistent ill health, or from frequent colds and 'flu, doing something about it will be high on your priority list. We saw in the first part of the book how your own internal ch'i needs to be in balance; the Chinese use acupuncturists to balance the ch'i within and many Westerners now visit acupuncturists as well. But whatever you do about your inner ch'i, the ch'i around you in your house and garden will also exert an influence. Although it cannot, on its own, effect a miracle cure for a serious illness, it can sometimes ease the symptoms, and it can create an environment in which minor complaints are less likely to flourish.

As before, the starting point is finding out where your health and happiness enrichment lies, what kind of ch'i it receives, and what remedy will be most effective against any negative ch'i.

House faces...	Health and happiness enrichment	Type of ch'i (positive/ negative)	Suitable remedy
South	South-west	Soothing/ disruptive	Straight lines
South-west	West	Changeable/ dangerous	Stillness
West	North-west	Expansive/ unpredictable	Sound
North-west	North	Nurturing/ lingering	Movement
North	North-east	Flourishing/ stagnating	Colour
North-east	East	Growing/ overpowering	Functional device
East	South-east	Creative/ provoking	Life
South-east	South	Vigorous/ accelerating	Light

A north-facing health and happiness enrichment, for example, is susceptible to lingering ch'i, which could make it difficult for you to shake off illnesses once you have fallen victim. Remedying the feng shui here will restore the nurturing ch'i which will nurse you back to health again.

A south-facing enrichment, on the other hand, will be prey to accelerating sha, and you may find that your illnesses often develop complications, and turn into worse conditions. Colds may become bronchitis, and perhaps even pneumonia, for example. Restoring the vigorous ch'i will give you the energy to fight the original illness before it progresses further.

Once you have established where your health and happiness enrichment lies, what sort of ch'i it attracts, and how to remedy the negative effects of it, you need to look at the room in general. As always, make sure it is bright, clean and tidy. Dark or messy corners where the ch'i can stagnate will correlate with aspects of your health which are never quite right – niggling back pain, frequent dull headaches or a tendency to blocked sinuses.

Visit this area of your house – and garden – frequently. Grow herbs in the health and happiness enrichment of your garden, and on the corresponding windowsills in the house if you can. Make sure this part of the house contains symbols of good health, happiness and fitness, such as pictures and statues of happy people, pots or jars of dried herbs associated with good health, pot pourri, representations of sunshine and water – both of which are essential life-giving sources of good health – and so on. This is also a good place to keep your first aid and medicine cupboard; make sure they are always restocked when necessary, and kept tidy.

You spend about a third of your life in bed, and whichever enrichment your bedroom falls in, any negative influences can affect your health. A beam across the bed, for example, can cause problems in the part of your body which it crosses. If it hangs over your stomach, you may be prone to sickness, nausea or digestive problems. If it is directly above your head, you may suffer from bad headaches or migraines.

Sometimes ch'i cannot get underneath your bed because your bed touches, or almost touches, the floor. This means that you cannot derive all the healing and refreshing energy which you should during sleep, and you will be more prone to lethargy. This will, in turn, weaken your resistance to illness and infection.

Feng shui and children

Children are at a stage in their lives when they are still growing and developing, and this makes them susceptible to the forces around them. This is how it should be; our job as parents is to mould and guide them as we think best, and their flexibility allows us to do this. However, it has its downside, too, because it means they are much more easily influenced by negative energies as well as positive ones. For this reason, good feng shui is especially important around children.

Start by establishing where the children and family enrichment is, and what kind of ch'i it attracts. Then apply the best type of remedy to ensure that you encourage the most positive ch'i.

House faces...	Children and family enrichment	Type of ch'i (positive/ negative)	Suitable remedy
South	North-east	Flourishing/ stagnating	Colour
South-west	East	Growing/ overpowering	Functional device
West	South-east	Creative/ provoking	Life
North-west	South	Vigorous/ accelerating	Light
North	South-west	Soothing/ disruptive	Straight lines
North-east	West	Changeable/ dangerous	Stillness
East	North-west	Expansive/ unpredictable	Sound
South-east	North	Nurturing/ lingering	Movement

Wherever your children enrichment falls, this is a good place to encourage your children to spend time. If it occupies your kitchen, make it welcoming for children – perhaps you could even put the television in there. If it is in the dining room, encourage them to work in there, or even swap the dining room and sitting room around so that this becomes your sitting room.

Children spend a huge amount of time in their bedrooms – even if they only sleep there they will still spend longer hours in there than adults do in their bedrooms. Many children also play, do their homework and entertain their friends in their bedroom. If you have more than one child's bedroom, you can't put all of them in the children and family enrichment, but put them in the most suitable enrichments you can, taking the child's nature into account. Here are a few examples:

- ■ If they are inclined to work too hard, put them in the pleasure and indulgence area.
- ■ If they are prone to illness, put them in health and happiness.
- ■ A child who doesn't socialise well would be suited to the friends and new beginnings enrichment, which would help them to socialise more easily.
- ■ If you have a child who never gets on with schoolwork, put their bedroom in the wisdom and experience part of the house.
- ■ A child who is shy could be encouraged out of their shell by sleeping in the fame enrichment.

Remember that the most nurturing ch'i comes from the Black Tortoise in the north, so your children will be well suited to the north of the house, or the east, the direction of the wise Green Dragon – or, of course, nestled between these two in the north-east.

Children's bedrooms

As well as putting your children in bedrooms which are in suitable enrichments, you should also lay the Pah Kwa octagon over each bedroom to see where is the best position for each piece of furniture. If children have a desk for schoolwork, put it in the wisdom and experience section of the room. Put the bed in health and happiness, or perhaps in children and family. If any sections of the Pah Kwa are missing from the room, hang a large mirror to represent the missing section, as we saw in Chapter 5.

One of the biggest problems in many children's bedrooms is that there is simply too much ch'i buzzing around because it is stirred up by electrical equipment. Get the television out of their bedrooms, and the CD player, and the computer. It's not unreasonable for them to want music in their rooms, but restrict them to a radio or simple CD or cassette player, not some huge piece of equipment which occupies a large chunk of the room. You should find that this results in a much calmer child.

If children share bedrooms, make sure that they each have their own personal space where the ch'i influences them alone. Otherwise they will feel they have no privacy or independence from their siblings. Avoid bunk beds if you possibly can; the child on the top will dominate the one who sleeps underneath. The child in the lower bunk will react either by becoming withdrawn, or by fighting back, which leads to conflict and unpleasantness. If you really haven't got the space, and have to use bunk beds, alternate which child sleeps in which bunk. Alternating on a nightly basis is disruptive, but alternate them on a weekly, monthly or even school-term basis.

Troubleshooting with feng shui and children

Any parent who says they've never had a single problem with their child is being, at best, economical with the truth. There is no end to the problems parents can encounter, but here are some of the more common ones, together with suggested remedies.

- *They never come home when they should.* Spruce up the bedroom, tidy it so the ch'i can circulate harmoniously, and put a ticking clock in the friends and new beginnings section of the room.

- *They won't tidy their room.* Tidy it for them the first time, and then give it a makeover to improve the flow of ch'i. Put a stillness remedy in the west, and a functional device in the east (where the ch'i can be overpowering), and add plenty of storage space, preferably in the wealth section of the room.

- *They spend all their time with their friends and never do their schoolwork.* Find some way of obstructing the friends and new beginnings enrichment in their room, and the pleasure and indulgence area, so that they devote less of their time to these aspects of their life. Put a piece of furniture here such as a wardrobe or chest of drawers where they don't spend too much time. Don't use a bed, chair or dressing table where they spend a lot of time.

- *They mope around all day watching television and never do anything worthwhile.* Liven up the ch'i in their room, and in the room where the television is, to encourage them to respond in kind. Decorate in a bright colour which suits the direction in which the room faces, and add plenty of life, light and movement remedies.

- *They just argue with you all the time.* Reduce conflict by making sure that all the furniture and other objects in their rooms are in a suitable enrichment. Create a link between their room and any enrichment over which the conflict arises. For example, if they argue over how much money you do or don't spend on them, link their room with your wealth enrichment by placing one object from a pair in each of the areas. Check your children and family enrichment – make sure it has good feng shui. If it is an area of excessive activity or friction, such as a utility room or garage, use remedies to calm it down.

■ *They are constantly devastated by one relationship problem after another.* This is a problem which afflicts many teenagers, and probably affected you once too, at least to some extent. You need to introduce some wisdom and experience into their relationship area by placing a functional device there (which represents wisdom and experience, as we saw in Chapter 5). You should also calm down their relationship area by making sure it contains nothing too full of energy, such as a radio, and no inappropriate symbols, such as a poster depicting someone crying.

■ *They spend money like water.* Move their piggy bank, or wherever they keep their money or building society passbook, to their wisdom and experience area, especially if it is currently in their pleasure and indulgence area (but don't expect miracles from teenagers – they're never going to save every last penny).

■ *The children don't get on with each other.* Make sure the rooms they spend time in together have good, calm feng shui. Decorate in restful colours which are appropriate to the direction they face. If the children share a room, give them each their own space within it. If they have separate rooms, encourage them to keep the doors open, at least when they are out, to help the ch'i move between the rooms. Link the rooms with colour or with objects which belong to the same group and are placed one in each room – give them each a matching cushion for their chair, and one of a pair or threesome of nesting tables.

Parenting is never going to be a doddle, but good feng shui can help to create a balanced environment in which it is far easier for children to grow up and for parents to support them. This, in turn, makes all the difficult bits far less complicated and overwhelming to deal with.

Feng shui, as we saw in Part One of this book, is a means of creating the most beneficial and positive energy around you, but it is also about plain common sense. It works on two levels; it harmonises the ch'i around you, and it focuses your concentration on the areas of your life that need attention. You and the natural energy of ch'i together can bring about changes greater than you would ever have thought possible.

FURTHER READING

Feng shui

An Anthropological Analysis of Chinese Geomancy, Stephen Feuchtwang, SMC, 1974.

Change your Life with Feng Shui, Li Pak Tin and Helen Yeap, Quantum, 1997.

Feng Shui, Angel Thompson, St Martin's Griffin, 1995.

Feng Shui, Kirsten M. Lagatree, Newleaf, 1996.

Feng Shui for Beginners, Richard Craze, Hodder & Stoughton, 1996.

Feng Shui in Your Garden, Roni Jay, Thorsons, 1998.

Feng Shui Made Easy, William Spear, Thorsons, 1995.

Interior Design with Feng Shui, Sarah Rossbach, Rider Books, 1987.

Practical Feng Shui, Richard Craze, Anness, 1997.

The Complete Illustrated Guide to Feng Shui, Lillian Too, Element Books, 1996.

The Elements of Feng Shui, Man-Ho Kwok with Joanne O'Brien, Element Books, 1991.

The Feng Shui Game Pack, Richard Craze, Godsfield Press and HarperCollins, 1997.

The Feng Shui Kit, Man-Ho Kwok, Piatkus, 1995.

The Feng Shui Pack, Richard Craze, Godsfield Press and HarperCollins, 1997.

The Living Earth Manual of Feng Shui, Chinese Geomancy, Stephen Skinner, Arkana, 1982.

The Western Guide to Feng Shui, Terah Kathryn Collins, Hay House Inc., 1995.

Chinese philosophy

Between Heaven and Earth, Harriet Beinfield and Efrem Korngold, Ballantine Books, 1991.

Chinese Astrology, Collins Gem, 1996.

Chinese Horoscopes for Beginners, Kristyna Arcarti, Hodder & Stoughton, 1995.

Chinese Mythology, Derek Walters, The Aquarian Press, 1992.

I Ching for Beginners, Kristyna Arcarti, Hodder & Stoughton, 1994.

Lao Tzu's TAO TE CHING, edited Timothy Freke, Piatkus, 1995.

Teach Yourself Chinese Astrology, Richard Craze, Hodder & Stoughton, 1997.

The Fundamental Principles of the Yi-king Tao, Veolita Parke Boyle, W & G Foyle, 1934.

The I Ching and Mankind, Diana ffarington Hook, Routledge and Kegan Paul, 1975.

The I Ching Workbook, R. L. Wing, Aquarian, 1983.

The Secret of the Golden Flower, Richard Wilhelm, Routledge and Kegan Paul, 1974.

The Way of Life, Witter Bynner, Perigee Books, 1944.

Chinese health

Chi Kung, James MacRitchie, Element, 1995.

Chinese Herbal Medicine, Richard Craze, Piatkus, 1996.

Teach Yourself Traditional Chinese Medicine, Richard Craze, Hodder & Stoughton, 1997.

The Complete Illustrated Guide to Chinese Medicine, Tom Williams, Element Books, 1997.

General

Cambridge Illustrated History of China, Patricia Buckley Ebrey, Cambridge University Press, 1996.

China, Land of Discovery and Invention, Robert Temple, Patrick Stephens, 1986.

Imperial China, Charis Chan, Penguin Books, 1991.

The Changing Society of China, Ch'u Chai and Winberg Chai, Mentor Books, 1962.

USEFUL ADDRESSES

United Kingdom

Feng Shui Network International
PO Box 2133
London W1A 1RL

Feng Shui Society
18 Alacross Road
London W5 4HT

Feng Shui Association
31 Woburn Place
Brighton
East Sussex BN1 9GA

The Feng Shui Company
Ballard House
37 Norway Street
Greenwich
London SE10 9DD

Australia

Feng Shui Design Studio
PO Box 705
Glebe
Sydney NSW 2037

Feng Shui Society of Australia
PO Box 1565
Rozelle
Sydney NSW 2039

North America

Earth Design
PO Box 530725
Miami Shore
Florida 33153

The Feng Shui Institute of America
PO Box 488
Wabasso
Florida 32970

Feng Shui Warehouse
PO Box 3005
San Diego
California 92163

Surf the Net with feng shui

At the time of writing there are some 5,968 relevant documents about feng shui on the Internet. These are but a few of them, selected to give you some addresses to get you started.

http://www.lmcinet.com/amfengshui
American Feng Shui Institute's Home Page web site.

http://www.ozemail.com.au/bmtv/fengshui.htm
Feng shui advice, videos, newsletters, remedies.

http://downtown.wcb.aol.com/ads/cats/cat_homegarden7txt.html
Home and garden feng shui, including bonsai trees.

http://www.spiritweb.org/Spirit/feng-shui-liu-07.html
Feng shui and love. Promotes spiritual consciousness on the Internet. Healing schools and techniques of feng shui and ch'i.

http://www.spiritweb.org/Spirit/feng-shui-liu-05.html
Feng shui and astrology.

http://www.fsgallery.com/
Feng shui gallery of calligraphy and art. A gallery of Chinese and Japanese art and calligraphy.

http://www.cwo.com/~ashlin/shui8.html
Feng Shui: The Chinese art of design and placement reviews. Two internationally sought-after consultants offer a history of this venerable art, and guidance on how to use it effectively.

http://www.mistral.co.uk/hammerwood/dowser.htm
Feng shui, earth acupuncture, geomancy, dowsing, geopathic stress, white and black streams, healing streams, ley lines, earth mysteries, earth healing, watercourses, underground water.

http://www.meltzerfengshui.com/
Creating heaven on earth. Carol Meltzer Feng Shui Designs. Functional Art Gallery.

http://www.cwo.com/~ashlin/flutes.html"
Feng shui flutes and word stones.

http://www.asiaconnect.com.my/lillian-too/fundamental/
Fundamentals of feng shui – the Trinity of Luck, Order and Form.

http://www.community.net/~sgxenja/index.html
Seann Xenja's home page. Welcome to the world of feng shui. The Web site of a feng shui consultant.

http://www.intersurf.com/locale/geo/
Geomancy Dragon Feng Shui Education Organisation.

INDEX